MEAT MAKES THE MEAL

by Margaret Deeds Murphy

DORISON HOUSE PUBLISHERS, INC., NEW YORK

About the Author

Margaret Deeds Murphy, author and Home Economist, was born in Strombsburg, Nebraska, received her Home Economics degree from the University of Nebraska in 1937, and has been cooking, testing, and writing about food ever since. She is the author of several cookbooks, has been associate food editor of Woman's Home Companion magazine, and was the head of the Recipe Test Kitchen of General Foods Corporation. Maggie Murphy lives with her husband on Cape Cod, where she operates a test kitchen for the development of recipes. She is currently preparing the food pages for Gray's Sporting Journal.

Cover art & chapter illustrations: Brian Cody
Book design: Cachalot Design Group   Marblehead, Massachusetts
Other illustrations (meat charts, etc.):
courtesy of National Live Stock and Meat Board

Copyright © 1977 by Dorison House Publishers, Inc.
Published by Dorison House Publishers, Inc.
183 Madison Avenue, New York, N.Y. 10016

ISBN: 0-916752-11-9

Library of Congress Number: 77-71479

Manufactured in the United States of America

I officially entered the meat packing business in 1911 when I was 16 years old, serving my apprenticeship in the retail market stall of the William Schluderberg & Son Company founded by my grandfather in 1858. In 1920 the company merged with the Thomas J. Kurdle Company, and the Schluderberg Kurdle Co., Inc. (Esskay) was founded.

Our beginnings were small but we have grown to the point where we now have many employees and utilize the most modern production techniques. This has come about, because we continue to be as dedicated, as our founders, to the concept of quality and service. Some members of both families are still active in the management of our business.

We are publishing this cookbook to help you add variety to your meals at home. In this book we have included not only the basics of meat cooking but how meat can be prepared for "fun time" eating. Today the whole family can participate in meal preparation and enjoy the benefits of wholesome delicious meat meals. I am sure that this book can help.

T. E. Schluderberg

CONTENTS

STORE TO STORAGE

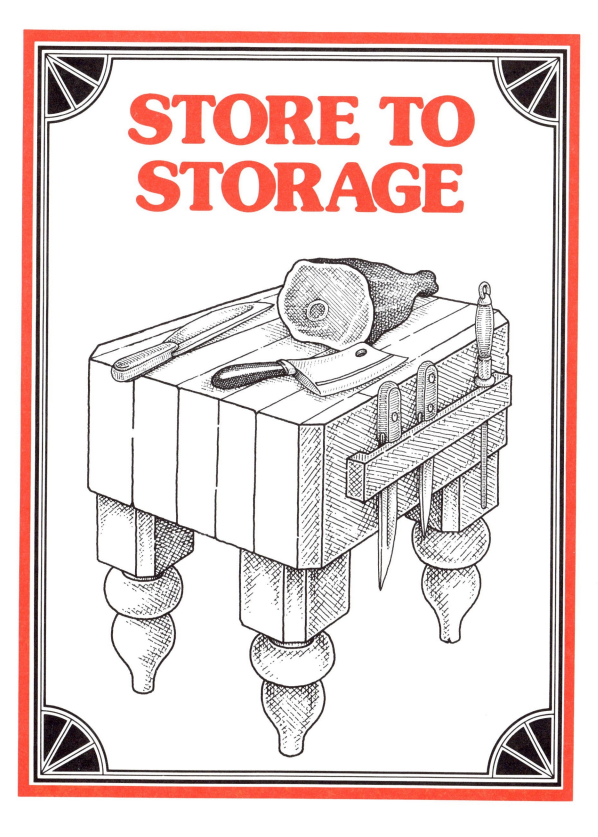

Introduction

Meat is basic. Meat is popular. Meals are planned around the meat to be served. Some combinations have even become classic because of their use through the years. Ham and pineapple, pork and apple sauce, lamb and mint jelly, to name a few. Meat is good for us as well as good to eat. It is a source of complete proteins, essential for proper growth and maintenance of the body.

This book from Esskay is planned to give help in buying, cooking and menu planning for the most common and some of the less common meat cuts and meat products.

Measurements in the book are given in both standard and metric, so that the book will be of continued value when only metric measurements are the standard. By the time metric measurements are in full use there will be metric measuring cups and spoons. Some cups, already marked for both measurements, are on the market now. A metric conversion chart is also included.

Buying Meats

When you go into the meat section of your supermarket, or if you have the services of a neighborhood meat store, the array of meat can be confusing particularly if you are new at the job of buying for a family. It's too easy to end up with the ever popular hamburger, which can get to be a bore even if you do have 100 recipes for preparing ground meat.

These charts show basic retail cuts of meat. They indicate the section from which the cuts come, and the identifying bones in the various cuts. If you can learn to know the bone formation in the various cuts it will help you to save money and get the right cut for the recipe when purchasing meat. Except, of course, for ground beef and cut up stew meat, one can even learn to know boneless cuts by the conformation, texture and the shape of the cut.

BEEF CHART

Chuck — Rib — Short Loin — Sirloin — Round

Fore Shank — Brisket — Short Plate — Flank — Tip

VEAL CHART

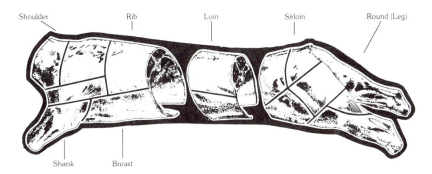

LAMB CHART

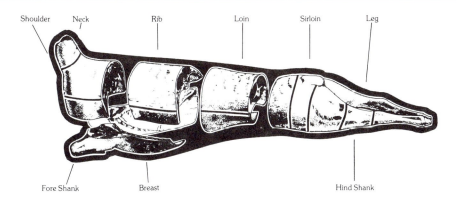

PORK CHART

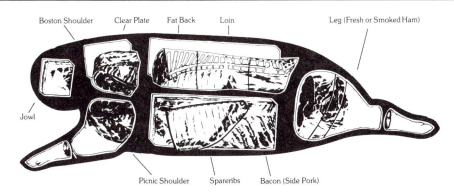

Always buy the best quality of meat you can afford. It will pay in the long run in good meals for your family.

In buying meat, purchases should be made according to use. As an example, do not buy expensive sirloin for stew when chuck or shoulder meat will cost less and be more tasty for that purpose.

The rib, loin, sirloin and top of the round are the more tender cuts which can be cooked by broiling, roasting, pan broiling or pan frying.

The remaining cuts, generally speaking, are better when cooked with moist heat, ground or marinated or tenderized before cooking.

The most efficient way to buy meat is to calculate the cost per serving. A piece with a lot of bone, oxtails are a good example, may cost less per pound, but with such a large proportion of bone, as in oxtails, no more than 2 servings per pound are possible. A boneless piece that costs twice as much, but which will make 4 servings per pound, costs the same per serving.

In calculating cost per serving take into account both bone and fat.

This chart will give you a quick idea of cost per serving at different price levels.

Cost per Pound	Servings per pound of meat			
	1½	2	3	4
.59	.39	.30	.20	.15
.69	.46	.35	.23	.17
.79	.53	.40	.26	.20
.89	.59	.45	.30	.22
.99	.66	.50	.33	.25
1.09	.73	.55	.36	.27
1.19	.79	.60	.40	.30
1.29	.86	.65	.43	.32
1.39	.93	.70	.46	.35
1.49	.99	.75	.50	.37
1.59	1.06	.80	.53	.40
1.69	1.13	.85	.56	.42
1.79	1.19	.90	.60	.45
1.89	1.26	.95	.63	.47
1.99	1.33	1.00	.66	.50
2.09	1.39	1.05	.70	.52
2.19	1.46	1.10	.73	.55
2.29	1.53	1.15	.76	.57
2.39	1.59	1.20	.80	.60
2.49	1.66	1.25	.83	.62
2.59	1.73	1.30	.86	.65

Other tips on buying include watching for specials. When a special is particularly appealing, buy what you can normally use for one or two meals, and then a little extra to freeze for future use.

It is also a good idea to have the complete menu in mind when buying meat. It will help you to have something which complements that particular meat, and make for more interesting meals.

The beef, lamb and veal government grades which are most likely to be found in the meat market are Prime, Choice and Good. This grade is stamped by a roller stamp with vegetable-based marking fluid the full length of the carcass or cut. You may also see signs in the market advertising "aged" beef, lamb or mutton. Usually only ribs and loins of high quality meat are aged. Aging tenderizes and gives the meat a characteristic aged flavor. Prime grade and aged beef command the highest prices.

The appearance of fresh meat is an important guide to its quality. Good quality beef is a uniform, bright light to deep red; veal is grayish pink, and lamb is pinkish red in color. Fine-textured firm lean meat is preferable to coarse-textured soft lean. The fat color will vary and is not an indication of quality. The bones of good quality meat are red and porous.

Care of Meat

Fresh meat should be brought home at once from the market and stored in the coldest place in the refrigerator for no more than 2 days before use. For longer storage, use the freezer. If it is prepackaged by the meat retailer it can be stored in that package. Fresh meat — not prepackaged — should be wrapped loosely in wax paper or aluminum foil to allow the air to circulate around the meat, for refrigerator storage. (You may just loosen the store wrapping). Some refrigerators have compartments for storing fresh meat unwrapped.

Meat to be frozen should be packaged tightly in vapor-moisture proof freezer wrap, polyethylene bags, or heavy-weight aluminum foil, and sealed, labeled and dated. Fresh meat properly wrapped will store at 0°F ($-18°C$) for 6 to 8 months. Cured meats such as ham, bacon and similar meats should not be frozen longer than a month for optimum flavor.

The ice cube section of your refrigerator does not usually reach 0°F ($-18°C$), so don't plan to keep foods frozen in there for long periods.

You may refreeze meat if it still has ice crystals, or if it is still cold and has not been kept at refrigerator temperatures for longer than one or two days. Keep in mind that refreezing may reduce the quality of products. Defrosted frozen meat should be given the same care as fresh meat.

Cured, smoked and luncheon-type meats have a little longer refrigerator life than fresh meats. They should be stored in the refrigerator, in the coldest place, unless the label specifies otherwise. They can be stored from 4 days up to a week. They should be wrapped in wax paper or aluminum foil to prevent interchange of flavors in the refrigerator. Most canned hams should be stored in the refrigerator or in a cool place, unless otherwise specified on the label.

Always treat meat with loving care. It is one of our most valuable foods.

Cooking frozen meats

When cooking most frozen meat, it is usually best to completely defrost before cooking. For best results meat should be defrosted in the refrigerator. Then cook it just as you would fresh meat. In broiling steaks, however, it has been found that there is less loss of juices if the steaks are not completely thawed. When you need to cook meat from the frozen state, add about ⅓ or ¼ more time than usual, depending on the thickness of the cut. If you have a microwave oven, directions for fast defrosting are included with the instructions.

STORAGE TIME CHART

Meat	Refrigerator (36 to 40°F) (2.2 to 4.4°C)	Freezer (0°F) (−18°C)
Fresh Beef	2 to 4 days	6 to 12 months
Fresh Veal	2 to 4 days	6 to 9 months
Fresh Pork	2 to 4 days	3 to 6 months
Fresh Lamb	2 to 4 days	6 to 9 months
Ground Beef, Veal, Lamb	1 to 2 days	3 to 4 months
Ground Pork	1 to 2 days	1 to 3 months
Specialty (or Variety) Meats	1 to 2 days	3 to 4 months
Luncheon Meats	1 week	1 or 2 weeks
Fresh Pork Sausage	1 week	60 days
Smoked Sausage	3 to 7 days	60 days
Dry and Semi-dry Sausage, unsliced	2 to 3 weeks	60 days
Frankfurters	4 to 5 days	1 month
Bacon	5 to 7 days	1 month
Smoked ham, whole	1 week	60 days
Smoked ham slices	3 to 4 days	60 days
Beef, corned	1 week	2 weeks
Leftover cooked meat	4 to 5 days	2 to 3 months

Frozen Combination Foods

Meat		Freezer
Meat Pies, cooked		3 months
Swiss Steak, cooked		3 months
Stews, cooked		3 to 4 months
Prepared meat dinners		2 to 6 months

The times given above for freezer storage do not mean that the meat cannot be used after that time. It means that after the time specified, the quality of the frozen product will not be at its optimum.

Freeze-Dried Meats

One of the outgrowths of the space age is freeze-dried products. In this process the meat is frozen and dehydrated at low temperatures, producing a dry but porous product. The meat retains its shape and can be rehydrated simply by placing it in water. After rehydration, the meat is cooked as if it were fresh. These products are of special interest to campers and outdoorsmen. The storage life is one to two years if kept packaged. No refrigeration is required.

Use manual machines rather than small electrical appliances; use small electric appliances in place of larger ones which require more energy.

MEATS THAT MAKE THE MEAL

STICK TO YOUR RIBS RECIPES
FOR STEAKS, ROASTS AND CHOPS

A fine steak or a roast prime rib of beef have never lost their glamour when a celebration is in order. To learn to cook steaks, roasts and chops to suit your taste is a rewarding project.

Since steaks, roasts and chops are cut from the rib, loin, sirloin and high quality leg of the beef, lamb, veal or pork, they can be cooked by open pan roasting and broiling or pan frying.

For roasting, one of the best investments you can make is a meat thermometer. A proper meat thermometer will give you the temperatures for roasting each kind of meat to the desired state of doneness, eliminating guesswork. Pork should always be well done, but beef, lamb or veal can be cooked to your own taste. A meat thermometer is easy to use — the only caution, insert it into the fleshy part of the meat so that it does not touch bone. Bone transfers the heat more rapidly and will give a false reading. Avoid fat, also.

The other pieces of equipment — a flat pan with a 2 or 3-inch (5 or 7.5 cm) rim — the broiler pan from your oven would do — and a rack on which to put the meat. The broiler rack could be used — but a V-rack or one that puts the meat down in the pan is a good investment since it can also be used for chicken and turkey and other fowl.

Slow oven roasting, 300 to 350°F (150 to 175°C) will retain the juices and produce a more flavorful and tender roast.

The meat can or cannot be seasoned with salt and pepper before roasting as you choose. Since it only penetrates about ¼-inch into the meat during cooking it does not affect flavor appreciably.

The meat should be placed on the rack with the fat side up so that the meat does its own basting, the thermometer inserted so that it does not touch bone.

Roasts are easier to carve if they are allowed to set 15 to 20 minutes after removal from the oven. The meat continues to cook from retained heat so remove from oven while meat thermometer is 5–10° below the required doneness.

Essential to proper carving is a well sharpened knife.

To make the gravy to serve with roast meats:

AU JUS — SERVED WITH ROAST RIB OF BEEF.

Pour off as much of the fat as possible from the roasting pan, but not the juice. It may be necessary to use a spoon to remove most of the fat. Add about 1½ cups (375 ml) of water to the juices in the pan and scrape loose any browned crust clinging to the pan. Season to taste with salt and freshly ground pepper — (some people might like to add a dash of Worcestershire or thick steak Sauce). Heat to boiling and pass with the beef in a gravy boat or bowl.

THICKENED GRAVY WITH ROASTS.

Pour off fat from the roasting pan, leaving about 2 tablespoons (30 ml) for each cup of gravy. Add 2 tablespoons (30 ml) of flour for each 2 tablespoons (30 ml) fat and scrape loose any browned crust clinging to the pan. Remove from heat and pour in 1½ cups (375 ml) cold water for each 2 tablespoons (30 ml) fat and flour. Cook and stir until boiling and thickened. Season to taste with salt and freshly ground pepper. If the gravy does not taste rich enough, add 1 or 2 bouillon cubes before seasoning.

Steaks and chops can be broiled or pan broiled. Beef suitable for broiling includes beef rib steak, porterhouse, sirloin, beef rib eye, tenderloin and ground beef patties. If of good quality beef, some chuck steaks can be broiled, but marinating or tenderizing will help to make them more tasty. Lamb chops, rib, arm, sirloin and loin all can be broiled. Bacon and Canadian-style bacon, center ham cut, rib pork chops, smoked pork loin chops can also be broiled.

Broiling means cooking the meat by direct heat. Steaks and chops to be broiled should be at least 1-inch (2.5 cm) thick. Pan broiling is cooking meat in a heavy frying pan or grill with little or no added fat and no cover. Generally speaking, meats to be pan broiled should be cut less than 1-inch (2.5 cm) thick.

Meat should be placed on a rack in the broiler pan and spaced 2 to 3 inches (5–7.5 cm) from source of heat. If the meat is cut up to 2-inches (5 cm) thick it should be placed 3 to 5 inches (7.6–10 cm) away. The broiler may or may not be preheated.

The charts give you an idea of the timing for the various cuts. The times are total times. The meat should be turned at the half point in the time given.

When cooking meats in a microwave oven follow the directions that come with your oven. There are differences in various brands of ovens, so that general directions cannot be given.

CHARTS FOR ROASTING AND BROILING*

Cut	Approximate Weight	Oven Temperature	Approximate Cooking Minutes Per Pound (.45 kg)
ROAST BEEF			
Rib, standing 6 to 7 inches (15 to 17.5 cm)	6 to 8 pounds (2.3–3.3 kg)	300–320°F. (150–160°C.)	rare 23–25 min. med. 27–30 min. well 32–35 min.
from backbone to rib end	4 to 6 pounds (1.8–2.7 kg)	same	rare 26–32 min. med. 34–38 min. well 40–42 min.
Rolled rib	5 to 7 pounds (2.25–3.15 kg)	same	rare 32 min. med. 38 min. well 48 min.

Cut	Approximate Weight	Oven Temperature	Approximate Cooking Minutes Per Pound (.45 kg)
Rib eye	4 to 6 pounds (1.8–2.7 kg)	350°F. (175°C.)	rare 18–20 min. med. 20–22 min. well 22–24 min.
Tenderloin, whole	4 to 6 pounds (1.8–2.7 kg)	425°F. (220°C.)	rare 45 to 60 min. total
Boneless rolled rump (high quality beef)	4 to 6 pounds (1.8–2.7 kg)	300 to 325°F. (150–160°C.)	cook to 150–170°F. (66–75°C.) 25-30 min.
Tip (high quality beef)	3½ to 4 pounds (1.58–1.8 kg)	300 to 325°F. (150–160°C.)	cook to 140–170°F. (60–75°C.) 35–40 min.
	4 to 6 pounds (1.8–2.7 kg)	300 to 325°F.	cook to 140–170°F. (60–75°C.) 30–35 min.
ROAST VEAL			
Leg	5 to 8 pounds (2.25–3.3 kg)	300 to 325°F. (150–160°C.)	cook to 170°F. (75°C.) 25–35 min.
Loin	4 to 5 pounds (1.8–2.7 kg)	same	30–35 min.
Rib (rack)	3 to 5 pounds (1.35–2.25 kg)	same	35–40 min.
Boneless shoulder	4 to 6 pounds (1.8–2.7 kg)	same	40–45 min.
ROAST FRESH PORK			
Loin, center	3 to 5 pounds (1.35–2.25 kg)	325 to 350°F. (160–175°C.)	30–35 min.
Loin, half	5 to 7 pounds (2.25–3.15 kg)	same	35–40 min.
Blade loin or sirloin	3 to 4 pounds (1.35–1.8 kg)	same	40–45 min.

Cut	Approximate Weight	Oven Temperature	Approximate Cooking Minutes Per Pound (.45 kg)
Boneless double	3 to 5 pounds (1.35−2.25 kg)	same	35−45 min.
Arm picnic shoulder	5 to 8 pounds (2.25−3.3 kg)	same	30−35 min.
Arm picnic shoulder, boneless	3 to 5 pounds (1.35−2.25 kg)	same	35−40 min.
, cushion	3 to 5 pounds (1.35−2.25 kg)	same	30−35 min.
Blade Boston shoulder	4 to 6 pounds (1.8−2.7 kg)	same	40−45 min.
Fresh ham Whole, bone in	12 to 16 pounds (5.4−7.2 kg)	same	22−26 min.
Whole, boneless	10 to 14 pounds (4.5−6.3 kg)	same	24−28 min.
Half, bone in	5 to 8 pounds (2.25−3.3 kg)	same	35−40 min.
Spareribs		same	1½ to 2 hours, total time

ROAST SMOKED PORK

Cut	Approximate Weight	Oven Temperature	Approximate Cooking Minutes Per Pound (.45 kg)
Ham (cook before eating) whole	10 to 14 pounds (4.5−6.3 kg)	300 to 325°F. (150−160°C.)	18−20 min.
half	5 to 7 pounds (2.25−3.15 kg)	same	22−25 min.
Shank or rump portion	3 to 4 pounds (1.35−1.8 kg)	same	35−40 min.
Ham, fully cooked	allow approximately 15 minutes per pound for heating whole ham to be served hot	300 to 325°F. (150−160°C.)	
Ham, fully cooked, half	5 to 7 pounds (2.25−3.15 kg)	325°F. (160°C.)	18−24 min.
Arm picnic shoulder	5 to 8 pounds (2.25−3.6 kg)	300 to 325°F. (150−160°C.)	35 min.

Cut	Approximate Weight	Oven Temperature	Approximate Cooking Minutes Per Pound (.45 kg)
Shoulder roll	2 to 3 pounds (0.9–1.35 kg)	300 to 325°F. (150–160°C.)	35–40 min.
Canadian-style Bacon	2 to 4 pounds (0.9–1.8 kg)	325°F. (160°C.)	35–40 min.
ROAST LAMB			
Leg	5 to 8 pounds (2.25–3.6 kg)	300 to 325°F. (150–160°C.)	rare 20–25 min. med. 25–30 min. well 30–35 min.
Shoulder	4 to 6 pounds (1.8–2.7 kg)	same	med. 25–30 min. well 30–35 min.
, boneless	3 to 5 pounds (1.35–2.25 kg)	same	40–45 min.
, cushion	3 to 5 pounds (1.35–2.25 kg)	same	30–35 min.
Rib (rack)	1½ to 3 pounds (0.65–1.35 kg)	375°F. (190°C.)	rare 30–35 min. med. 35–40 min. well 40–45 min.

*Internal temperature when removed from oven for rare: 140°F. (60°C.)
medium: 160°F. (70°C.)
well: 170–180°F. (75–85°C.)

Cut	Weight or Thickness	Approximate Cooking Time	
		Rare	Medium
BROILED BEEF			
Rib eye steak			
1-inch (2.5 cm)	8 to 10 oz. (225–280 gm)	15 min.	20 min.
1½-inch (3.75 cm)	12 to 14 oz. (340–400 gm)	25 min.	30 min.
2-inch (50 cm)	16 to 20 oz. (0.45–0.56 kg)	35 min.	45 min.

Cut	Weight or Thickness	Approximate Cooking Time	
		Rare	Medium
Top loin steak			
1-inch (2.5 cm)	1 to 1½ pounds (0.45 to 0.675 kg)	15 min.	20 min.
1½-inch (3.75 cm)	1½ to 2 pounds (0.675 – 0.9 kg)	25 min.	30 min.
2-inch (5.0 cm)	2 to 2½ pounds (0.9 – 1.13 kg)	35 min.	45 min.
Sirloin steak			
1-inch (2.5 cm)	1½ to 3 pounds (0.675 – 1.35 kg)	20 min.	25 min.
1½-inch (3.75 cm)	2¼ to 4 pounds (1.01 – 1.8 kg)	30 min.	35 min.
2-inch (5.0 cm)	3 to 5 pounds (1.35 – 2.25 kg)	40 min.	45 min.
Porterhouse			
1-inch (2.5 cm)	1¼ to 2 pounds (0.56 – 0.9 kg)	20 min.	25 min.
1½ inch (3.75 cm)	2 to 3 pounds (0.9 – 1.35 kg)	30 min.	35 min.
2-inch (5 cm)	2½ to 3½ pounds (1.1 – 1.575 kg)	40 min.	45 min.
Filet Mignon			
1-inch (2.5 cm)	4 to 6 oz. (112 – 168 gm)	15 min.	20 min.
1½-inch (3.75 cm)	6 to 8 oz. (168 – 224 gm)	18 min.	22 min.
Ground beef patties 1 inch (2.5 cm) thick by 3-inch (7.5 cm)	4 oz. (112 gm)	15 min.	25 min.

BROILED SMOKED PORK

Cut	Weight or Thickness	Rare	Medium
Ham slice			
½-inch (1.25 cm)	¾ to 1 pound (336 – 448 gm)	Always cooked well done.	10 to 12 min.
1-inch (2.5 cm)	1½ to 2-pounds (0.675 – 0.9 kg)		16 to 20 min.
Loin chops			
¾ to 1-inch thick (2 – 2.5 cm)			15 to 20 min.

21

Cut	Weight or Thickness	Approximate Cooking Time	
		Rare	Medium
Canadian-style Bacon			
¼-inch slices (.625 cm)			6 to 8 min.
½-inch (1.25 cm)			8 to 10 min.
Bacon			4 to 5 min.
BROILED FRESH PORK			
Rib or Loin chops	¾ to 1-inch (2−2.5 cm)	Always cooked well done.	20 to 25 min.
Shoulder steaks	½ to ¾-inch (1.25−2 cm)		25 to 30 min.
BROILED LAMB			
Shoulder chops			
1-inch (2.5 cm)	5 to 8 oz. (140−224 gm)		12 min.
1½-inch (3.75 cm)	8 to 10 oz. (224 to 280 gm)		18 min.
2-inch (5 cm)	10 to 16 oz. (280−448 gm)		22 min.
Rib chops			
1-inch (2.5 cm)	3 to 5 oz. (84 to 140 gm)		12 min.
1½-inch (3.75 cm)	8 to 10 oz. (224−280 gm)		18 min.
2-inch (5 cm)	6 to 10 oz. (168−280 gm)		22 min.
Loin chops			
1-inch (2.5 cm)	4 to 7 oz. (112−196 gm)		12 min.
1½ inch (3.75 cm)	6 to 10 oz. (168−280 gm)		18 min.
2-inch (5 cm)	8 to 14 oz. (224−392 gm)		22 min.
Ground lamb patties			
1-inch (2.5 cm) thick by 3-inch (7.5 cm) across	4 oz. (112 gm)		18 min.

Carving Meat

Roasted meats carve more easily if allowed to stand after coming from the oven. Rare roasts should be covered loosely and allowed to remain in the open oven or some other warm place for 20 to 30 minutes before carving. Medium and well done roasts should stand 10 to 15 minutes. Steaks and chops however, should be carved immediately.

Always remove strings or skewers used in preparing the roast before it leaves the kitchen.

Carving sets come as a standard set — which is a knife with a curved blade 8 to 9 inches (20 to 22.5 cm) long, a fork to match and may or may not have a steel for sharpening. A set with a blade from 6 to 7 inches (15 to 17.5 cm) long is a steak set. Both are nice to have but a standard set will do for both jobs. A roast slicer and a carver's helper are accessory pieces you might want to add to your carving equipment. There are also electric knives.

More important than the length of the knife is the sharpness of the blade. So learn either to sharpen the blade on a steel or have a good knife sharpener in the kitchen. No matter how tender the meat is, if the knife is dull it will not cut it. It is a good idea to sharpen individual steak knives every so often, too.

These are simple illustrations to give you the basic steps in carving some of the more common roasts and steaks.

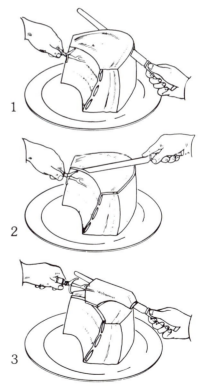

1

2

3

Standing Rib Roast　▶

1. With cut surface up and rib side to the left of carver, hold roast firmly with fork, guard up, inserted between two top ribs. Beginning at outside edge at large end of roast, draw knife across to the rib side cutting slice about three-eighths inch in thickness. 2. Loosen the slice by cutting along the bone with the tip of the knife. 3. As each slice is cut, steady it with the fork and lift it on the blade of the knife to one side of the platter, or to another hot platter, until enough slices have been cut to serve everyone.

Rolled Rib Roast

1

1. Insert fork at extreme left just below top of roast with guard up. The guard on the carving fork should always be up when the carver is cutting toward his left hand. As the slices are made the fork is taken out and inserted lower in the side of the roast. In making the slice, draw the knife from right to left. To make a smooth, even slice, care should be taken that the direction of the knife is not altered throughout carving. 2. Lift each slice on the blade of the knife, steadying it with the fork as it is placed on one side of the platter, or on another hot platter provided for this purpose. Before serving the individual plates, cut enough slices for every one at the table.

2

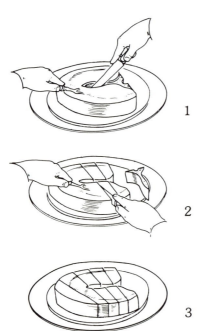

1

2

3

◀ Porterhouse Steak

1. Separate meat from bone by cutting down close to bone with point of knife. Remove bone to one side of platter. 2. Beginning at wide end of the steak and with knife at right angles to original position of bone, cut steak into sections about an inch wide, more or less, according to the number to be served. A piece of tenderloin and a piece of wide muscle should be served to each. 3. If flank end is to be served, carve it across the width of the muscle as this shortens the muscle fibers and makes a more desirable serving.

Blade Pot-Roast

1. Insert carving fork in left side of pot-roast. Following the dividing line between muscles, remove a small section of pot-roast, separating the meat from the bone. 2. Insert the fork in this small piece and turn so that the surface which was in a horizontal position is in a vertical one. 3. With fork in position, cut slices one-fourth to three-eighths of an inch thick. Proceed to separate other small pieces and carve in the same manner. This method enables the carver to slice across the grain of meat.

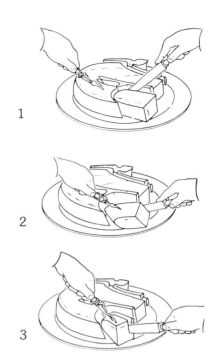

1

2

3

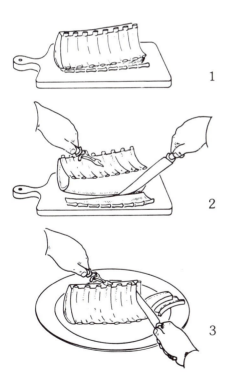

1

2

3

Loin of Pork

1. Remove back bone, which has been separated from the ribs by sawing across the ribs close to and parallel to back bone. The back bone loosens during roasting and is easily removed. 2. Before taking roast to the table remove back bone by cutting close to the back bone and at right angles to the ribs. 3. Place roast on platter with rib ends up and ribs toward the carver. Hold roast firmly with fork. Make first slice by drawing knife as close as possible to the left of the first rib; the second slice close to the right side of the second rib; the third slice to the left of the third rib and so on. Every other slice will contain a rib bone with a boneless slice cut from between each pair of ribs. With a large loin of pork, it is possible to cut two slices between each pair of ribs. In this way slices of the desired thickness may be secured. Two slices usually are served to each person.

25

Baked Whole Ham

1. Place ham with fat side up, shank end to carver's right. Cut two or three slices parallel to the length of the ham from the smaller meaty section. 2. Turn the ham so that it rests on the cut surface. Holding firmly with the fork, cut a small wedge shaped piece from the shank end. Then proceed to cut thin slices down to the leg bone until the aitch bone is reached. 3. With the fork still in place, release the slices by running the knife along the bone and at right angles to the slices. For additional servings, turn and carve other side of ham.

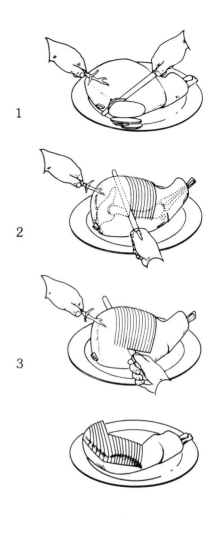

1

2

3

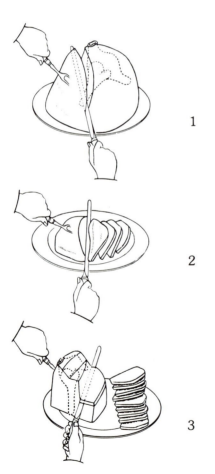

1

2

3

Rump Half of Ham

1. Place half of ham with face on carving board. Cut down along aitch-bone to remove boneless piece from side of ham. 2. Cut boneless piece (with freshly cut face on bottom) into cross-grain servings. 3. Hold remaining piece with fork and carve across meat until knife strikes aitch-bone. Release each slice from bone with tip of knife and lift it to side of platter.

Picnic Arm Shoulder

Carving is the same for both a roasted (baked) smoked picnic and a roasted (baked) fresh picnic.

1. Remove lengthwise slice as shown here. Turn picnic so that it rests on surface just cut. 2. Cut down to arm bone at a point near elbow bone. Turn knife and cut along arm bone to remove boneless arm meat. 3. Carve boneless arm meat by making perpendicular slices from top of meat down to cutting board. 4. Remove meat from each side of arm bone. Carve the two boneless pieces.

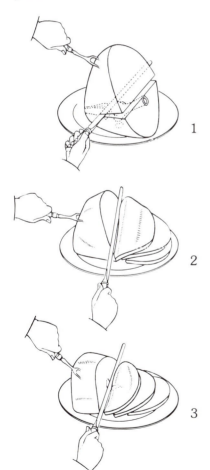

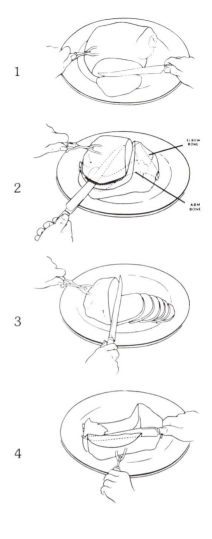

◀ **Shank Half of Ham**

1. With shank at carver's left, turn ham so thick cushion side is up. Cut along top of leg and shank bones and under fork to lift off boneless cushion. 2. Place cushion and meat on carving board and make perpendicular slices as illustrated. 3. Cut around leg bone with tip of knife to remove meat from this bone. Turn meat so that thickest side is down. Slice in same manner as cushion piece.

27

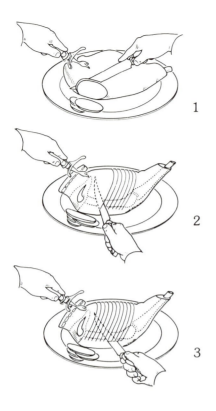

◀ Leg of Lamb

1. Place platter so that leg bone is to the carver's right. Insert the fork firmly in the large end of the leg and carve two or three lengthwise slices from the side nearest the carver. 2. Turn the leg so that it rests firmly on the surface just cut. Holding the roast firmly with the fork inserted to the left, and beginning at the shank end to the right, make the first slice down to the leg bone and continue to make slices parallel to this slice until the aitch bone at the large end is reached. The slices should be about one-fourth to three-eighths of an inch thick. 3. With the fork still in place the knife is run parallel to the leg bone to free slices all at one time.

Crown Roast of Lamb ▶

The crown roast of lamb or pork is carved in much the same way as the pork loin. Steady the crown by inserting the fork between the ribs to the carver's left. Make slice by cutting down through the center between each pair of ribs in the case of a crown of lamb, or at the left and right sides of the ribs in the case of a crown roast of pork. One chop and a portion of dressing or whatever vegetables that may be used to fill the crown are served to each person. Frequently a whole head of cauliflower, cooked separately, is placed in the center of the crown. This makes a very attractive service, but, before carving, it should be lifted to one side of the platter, so as not to interfere with carver.

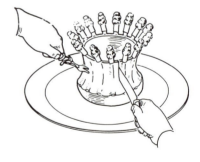

MEAT SEASONING CHART

Spices and Herbs

ALLSPICE	Beef, Ham, Lamb
BASIL	Beef, Veal, Lamb, Pork, Poultry
BAY LEAF	Beef, Veal, Lamb, Poultry
CARAWAY SEED	Beef, Lamb, Pork
CELERY SEED	Beef, Poultry
CHILI POWDER	Beef, Poultry
CLOVES	Ham, Pork
CUMIN	Beef, Poultry
CURRY	Beef, Veal, Lamb, Poultry
DILL	Lamb, Poultry
GARLIC	Beef, Lamb, Pork, Poultry
GINGER	Beef, Veal, Ham, Lamb, Pork, Poultry
MACE	Beef, Veal
MARJORAM	Beef, Veal, Lamb, Pork, Poultry
MINT	Veal, Lamb
MUSTARD	Beef, Veal, Ham, Pork, Poultry
OREGANO	Beef, Veal, Lamb, Pork, Poultry
ROSEMARY	Beef, Veal, Lamb, Pork, Poultry
SAFFRON	Poultry
SAGE	Veal, Lamb, Pork, Poultry
SAVORY	Beef, Veal, Lamb, Pork, Poultry
TARRAGON	Beef, Poultry
THYME	Beef, Veal, Lamb, Pork, Poultry

Herbs and spices liven the flavor of meats and poultry. Be discreet in their use. Begin with ¼ teaspoon (2 ml) dried herb for every 4 servings. Measure leaves and then crush dried herbs. Fresh herbs are snipped, rather than crushed, and you may use three times as much.

Remember that salt measurements in recipes are approximate. You should "salt to taste." Start by putting in less than the amount called for, and then add and taste. Salt should give the flavor of foods a lift, but the food shouldn't taste salty. And once you oversalt, there is nothing you can do about it.

But there are many recipes for steaks and roasts which incorporate seasonings. A sampling for the different kinds of meat is included.

STEAK AU POIVRE

This recipe at first glance looks complicated but it can be made less so by preparing the Brown Sauce in advance. If any sauce is left over be sure to save it for future use. It's good on hamburger steak or any meat. The peppered steak can also be made ready sometime earlier in the day. Serve baked potatoes and a green vegetable with the steak. A wedge of lettuce with French dressing makes a good salad.

Brown Sauce

¾ cup (180 ml) chopped mushrooms
2 tablespoons (30 ml) butter
¾ cup (180 ml) dry sherry

2 cups (500 ml) beef broth
1 tablespoon (15 ml) meat
 extract

Saute mushrooms in butter for 3 minutes. Add sherry and cook until reduced to half. Stir in broth and meat extract and cook over low heat about 15 minutes. Makes about 2 cups (500 ml).

Prepare the steaks:

4 boneless sirloin steaks
 about 2 pounds (0.90 kg)
2 to 3 tablespoons (30 to 45 ml)
 crushed peppercorns
3 tablespoons (45 ml) butter
2 tablespoons (30 ml) finely chopped
 shallots

½ ounce (14 g) cognac
1 cup (250 ml) dry red wine
2 cups (500 ml) brown sauce

Trim steaks of all fat and cut into serving pieces. Spread crushed peppercorns over both sides of steak, pressing into the meat with a mallet. Heat 2 tablespoons (30 ml) butter in skillet. Place the steaks in the hot butter and cook over medium heat 5 minutes on each side. Remove steaks from pan (keep hot) and pour out butter. Add shallots, let simmer 1 minute. Flame brandy in skillet and add red wine. Let reduce to ⅓ its volume. Add brown sauce and cook 5 minutes. Remove from heat and add remaining butter. Serve sauce with steak. Makes 4 servings.

Meat is the best source of iron necessary for healthy blood.

CHATEAUBRIAND

Chateaubriand has always been something special. The sauce can be made in advance and reheated over hot water. With Chateaubriand a casserole of Duchess Potatoes, new peas cooked in lettuce and Belgian endive with lemon and oil would be elegant.

Bearnaise Sauce

½ cup (125 ml) white wine
1 tablespoon (15 ml) tarragon vinegar
2 teaspoons (10 ml) chopped shallots
1 small sprig parsley

2 peppercorns
2 egg yolks, beaten
4 tablespoons (60 ml) butter

Combine wine, vinegar and seasonings. Bring to a boil and simmer 5 minutes. Strain. Put egg yolks in top of double boiler and gradually beat in hot wine, then butter, 1 tablespoon at a time. Cook over hot water, stirring constantly until mixture is quite thick. Remove from water and cover. Makes about ¾ cup (180 ml).

Have beef tenderloin cut into steaks thick enough to weigh 1 pound (0.45 kg) each. Broil about 3-inches (7.5 cm) from heat 15 minutes for rare, 20 minutes medium, turning to cook both sides.

Arrange steaks on hot platter and serve with Bearnaise sauce. One steak should serve two.

STEAK DINA

Steak Dina has to be last minute cooking (except for having the steaks pounded thin earlier) so avoid last minute preparation for the rest of the meal. Creamy scalloped potatoes and a dish of Julienne carrots can both be oven cooked. A relish tray of cherry tomatoes, radishes and celery sticks would serve as salad.

1 14 ounce (392 gm) boneless sirloin
   steak, trimmed of fat
2 tablespoons (30 ml) butter
Olive oil
½ teaspoon (2 ml) dry mustard
2 teaspoons (10 ml) chopped chives

Salt, freshly ground pepper
   to taste
1 teaspoon (5 ml) Worcestershire
   sauce
1 tablespoon (15 ml) lemon juice
1 teaspoon (5 ml) chopped parsley

Pound meat with a mallet until very thin.

Heat 1 tablespoon (15 ml) butter with a few drops of olive oil in a 10-inch (25.0 cm) skillet. Add mustard and chives. Season steak with salt and pepper and brush with oil. Add to butter mixture and cook quickly (1½ to 2 minutes on each side). Remove steaks to warm plate. Add Worcestershire sauce, lemon juice, parsley and remaining butter. Blend quickly over low heat. Pour over steaks and serve. Makes 2 servings.

LONDON BROIL

Originally London Broil was always prepared from the flank steak. Now it is more likely to be a boneless cut of beef from the shoulder or leg of the beef. After broiling to suit the taste, it should be sliced on the bias in thin slices with a very sharp slicing knife. It may or may not be marinated in a seasoned mixture. I like to spread the steak with butter and Worcestershire sauce (this does not work very well for BBQ cooking) before broiling. Mashed potatoes always seem to go well with London Broil and buttered broccoli. Then serve a lettuce and tomato tossed salad.

1 boneless steak, about 3 pounds
   (1.35 kg)
1 cup (250 ml) salad oil
4 tablespoons (60 ml) vinegar
1 clove garlic, mashed

½ teaspoon (2 ml) salt
Fresh ground pepper to taste
½ teaspoon (2 ml) dry thyme

Trim off any fat from steak. Mix remaining ingredients. Pour over steak in a shallow pan or, using a leak proof plastic bag, put steak in bag, add marinade and close tightly with a tie. Marinate from 6 hours to overnight in the refrigerator.

To broil, remove steak from marinade. Broil 2 to 3 inches (5 to 7.5 cm) from heat, about 20 minutes, turning once. Slice on bias in thin slices to serve. Makes 6 servings.

STEAK AND VEGETABLES

Plain cooked rice or a pilaf and a salad of endive could complete this meal.

2 pounds (0.9 kg) sliced tenderloin
4 tablespoons (60 ml) butter
   or margarine
2 tablespoons (30 ml) oil
1 teaspoon (5 ml) salt
⅛ teaspoon (0.5 ml) chili powder
⅛ teaspoon (0.5 ml) powdered
   sage
1 teaspoon (5 ml) coarsley crushed
   black peppercorns
½ pound (0.225 kg) fresh mushrooms

1 clove garlic, minced
1 medium onion, coarsely chopped
1 large green pepper, coarsely diced
2 tomatoes, peeled and diced
2 tablespoons (30 ml) tomato paste
½ cup (125 ml) soy sauce
2 tablespoons (30 ml) wine vinegar

Pan fry tenderloin in half butter and half oil over high heat with salt, chili powder, sage and pepper until it is medium rare. With a slotted spoon, transfer to a 2½ quart (2 L) buttered stove top casserole. Wash and quarter mushrooms. Add remaining butter and oil to skillet and quickly pan fry vegetables about 5 minutes, stirring. Add tomato paste, soy sauce and vinegar. Stir into meat in casserole. Heat together about 10 minutes. Vegetables should not be overcooked. Makes 6 servings.

MIXED GRILL COMBINATIONS

In cooking a mixed grill, put the piece of meat on broiler that takes longest time first, then work backwards with the timing.

Steak fillets, mushroom caps, tomato slices

Lamb chops, sausages, pineapple slices, par boiled sweet potato slices

Ham slice, par boiled sweet potato slices, apple rings sprinkled with brown sugar

Fillets of beef, mushroom caps

Calves liver, sausages, peach half with cranberry sauce

Ground beef patties, tomato slices, potato slices dipped in butter or margarine

BEEF WELLINGTON *

In which a 5 pound (2.25 kg) beef tenderloin is baked then rebaked in a pastry crust. It is a dish which takes a little time and patience — but is quite spectacular. It can be served hot or cold and makes a stunning centerpiece on a buffet filled with food. Fresh asparagus, hollandaise, Bib lettuce salad would go well with Beef Wellington served hot.

Step 1.   **Puff Paste**

1 lb (0.45 kg) sweet butter	1 teaspoon (5 ml) salt
4 cups (1000 ml) unsifted all-purpose flour	1 cup (250 ml) ice water

Wash the butter, squeezing and kneading in a bowl of very cold water, until smooth and soft- (but not melting).

Sift the flour with salt into a mixing bowl. Work 2 tablespoons (30 ml) of the butter into the flour with the finger tips. Gradually stir in water using the hands. The mixture should be about the same texture as the butter, firm but not hard.

Place the dough on a lightly floured pastry cloth and roll into a rectangle ¼-inch (.625 cm) thick. Shape the butter into a flat, square piece about ½-inch (1.25 cm) thick and place on dough in the center. Fold one end over on the butter, the other over the dough, completely covering the butter. Press the side edges together and chill dough 15 minutes.

Place chilled dough on the pastry cloth with one of the side edges facing you and roll it out away from you to make another long rectangle. Be careful not to let the butter break through the pastry. (When the butter breaks through air is lost and this is what makes Puff Pastry puff.) Fold this rectangle into thirds — turn so side edge faces you and repeat rolling and turning twice. Then chill dough 15 – 20 minutes. Repeat rolling and turning two more times and then chill dough before rolling and cutting.

The Puff Pastry may be made the day before, wrapped carefully in plastic wrap and kept under refrigeration until ready to use. If any pastry is left over from making the crust for the Beef Wellington, wrap it in freezer wrap, seal and date and freeze for future use.

* continued

Step 2:   **Paté**

6 sprigs parsley   Dash allspice
3 large mushrooms   ¼ teaspoon (1 ml) salt
3 anchovy fillets   1 can (4 or 4½ ounce 112 or 126 gm)
6 celery leaves   liver paté
3 tablespoons (45 ml) chopped   ¼ cup (50 ml) dry sherry
  ripe olives   1 tablespoon (15 ml) butter
Dash nutmeg

Chop parsley, mushrooms, anchovy and celery leaves finely in blender. Combine with remaining ingredients in a small saucepan and cook over low heat 5 minutes, stirring constantly. Cool.

Step 3:

1 tenderloin of beef, about 5 pounds (2.25 kg)
3 tablspoons (45 ml) butter, softened

Place tenderloin on a rack in a pan and spread with butter. Roast at 425°F (220°C) 25 minutes. Remove from oven and cool.

Step 4:

Roll out part of the pastry into a rectangle that is about 1½-inches (3.75 cm) larger than the beef tenderloin. Transfer to a well buttered flat baking pan with a narrow edge. Place baked, cooled tenderloin in center of pastry and spread tenderloin with paté. Roll out another rectangle of pastry. Place over tenderloin and pinch pastry edges together to seal. Brush edges with beaten egg white before pinching to help seal. Cut out pieces of pastry in decorative shapes and fasten on top of pastry with egg white in a decorative manner. Brush pastry with egg yolk mixed with 1 or 2 tablespoons (15 or 30 ml) water. Bake at 400°F (200°C) about 30 minutes or until golden. Remove from oven and let stand about 15 minutes. Place on platter. Garnish with watercress. To serve, cut into slices about 1-inch (2.5 cm) thick. Makes about 10 – 12 servings.

Serve occasional meals by candlelight (increases romance).

ROAST PORK LOIN
WITH SPICY SAUCE

Bake potatoes (yams would be good) and casserole of creamed cabbage with the pork.

1 center cut pork loin (3 to 5
   pounds − 1.5 to 2.25 kg)
1 teaspoon (5 ml) salt
1 clove garlic, optional
Fresh ground pepper to taste
1 medium onion, finely diced
1 tablespoon (15 ml) Worcestershire sauce

1 tablespoon (15 ml) brown sugar
½ teaspoon (2 ml) paprika
2 tablespoons (30 ml) catsup
½ cup (125 ml) wine vinegar
¼ cup (50 ml) water

Put pork in roasting pan. Mix salt, garlic and pepper in mortar and pestle and rub over pork. Insert meat thermometer so that bulb reaches center of meat but does not touch bone. Roast at 325°F (160°C) for 1 hour. Meantime combine remaining ingredients and simmer 15 minutes. Use to baste roast the remainder of the cooking time (½ to 1 hour, depending on size of roast. Meat thermometer should read 170°F (75°C) when roast is done. Serve with any left over sauce. Makes 6 to 10 servings.

APRICOT STUFFED SHOULDER OF PORK

With Apricot Stuffed Shoulder of Pork serve baked sweet potatoes, mixed vegetable and sliced tomato salad.

Have the meat man remove the bone from a shoulder of pork. It should weigh from 3 to 5 pounds (1.5 to 2.25 kg). Fill the pocket formed from the boning with the following stuffing.

Apricot Stuffing

1¼ cups (300 ml) dried apricots
   cooked
1 cup (250 ml) soft bread crumbs
1 cup (250 ml) cracker crumbs
¼ cup (50 ml) diced celery

¼ cup (50 ml) shredded toasted
   almonds
1 teaspoon (5 ml) salt
Dash freshly ground pepper

Cut apricots into small pieces and lightly mix with all ingredients. Spoon into cavity of pork. Fasten opening with skewers (or sew). Place on rack in roasting pan and bake at 325°F (160°C) for 30 − 35 minutes per pound (0.45 kg) (about 2½ − 3 hours total time). Baste roast with pan juices while roasting. To serve, slice and serve dressing and meat. Makes 6 to 8 servings.

PORK CHOPS WITH CHESTNUTS

The onions and chestnuts give a special flair to the chops. Finish the menu with spaetzle or noodles, fresh asparagus and chilled apple sauce.

6 pork chops about 1-inch (2.5 cm)
    thick
2 tablespoons (30 ml) butter or
    margarine
8 small white onions, boiled

12 chestnuts boiled and peeled *or*
1 can (6 ounce – 168 gm) water
    chestnuts, drained
2 cups (500 ml) wine sauce

Trim fat from pork chops and cook in butter in a large skillet about 30 – 35 minutes over moderate heat, until pork chops are well done. Remove from skillet and keep hot. Add onions and chestnuts and wine sauce to skillet and heat thoroughly. Serve sauce with chops. Makes 6 servings.

Wine Sauce

1 small carrot, chopped
¼ cup (50 ml) chopped celery
1 clove garlic, minced
1 tablespoon (15 ml) butter or
    margarine
¼ cup (50 ml) flour

1 cup (250 ml) beef bouillon
¾ cup (180 ml) Chablis wine
1 tablespoon (15 ml) chopped parsley
1 bay leaf
6 peppercorns

Saute carrots, celery and garlic in butter until tender. Add flour and cook until browned. Stir in remaining ingredients and simmer 45 minutes. Strain. Makes about 2 cups.

HELEN'S BEST PORK CHOPS

Bake whole kernel corn and spinach in oven dishes with the pork. Add an apple salad.

6 pork chops, cut 1-inch (2.5 cm) thick
¼ cup (50 ml) milk
1 egg
½ – ¾ cup (125 ml – 180 ml) Italian
    flavored bread crumbs

4 tablespoons (60 ml) butter or
    margarine
6 large onions, sliced thin
1 teaspoon (5 ml) salt
Fresh ground pepper to taste

Trim fat from pork chops. Mix egg and milk in pie plate. Dip pork chops in egg and milk, then in bread crumbs. Heat butter in skillet and brown chops over medium-high heat. Put a layer of half the onions in a buttered casserole, then three of the chops, repeat. Sprinkle each layer with salt and pepper. Bake at 325°F (160°C) 1 hour or until chops are tender. Makes 6 servings.

1 boneless ready-to-eat ham
  (about 10 pounds (4.50 kg)

½ cup (125 ml) sherry wine
4 tablespoons (60 ml) honey

Bake ham 12 to 15 minutes per pound at 325°F. (160°C.) basting often with wine and honey which have been blended. Remove from oven and cool to lukewarm. While ham is cooling, prepare pastry.

Pastry:

6 cups (1500 ml) all purpose flour
3 teaspoons (15 ml) baking powder
1½ teaspoons (7.5 ml) salt
½ teaspoon (3 ml) powdered sage
½ teaspoon (3 ml) dry mustard

1¼ cups (325 ml) shortening
1 cup (250 ml) cold milk
½ cup (125 ml) ice water
2 egg yolks
2 tablespoons (30 ml) water

Sift flour with dry ingredients into a bowl. Cut in shortening using a pastry blender or 2 knives to form a mixture like coarse meal. Stir in milk and enough ice water with a fork until pastry follows the fork around the bowl.

Roll out half the pastry on a lightly floured board into a rectangle ¼ inch thick. Transfer to an ungreased shallow baking pan about 15 x 10 inches (37.5 x 25.0 cm). Center ham on pastry in pan. Roll out remaining pastry and drape over top of ham. Trim any excess and fit pastry around ham snugly and pinch together where pieces meet. Cut a one-inch (2.5 cm) hole in top to vent steam.

Mix together egg yolks and 2 tablespoons (30 ml) water and brush lightly over pastry. To decorate, cut small shapes from pastry trimmings. Dip in egg yolk mixture and arrange on pastry as desired. Bake at 425°F. (220°C.) 30 to 35 minutes or until ham is nicely browned. To insure even browning, check during baking to see if any spots were missed with glaze and brush again. To serve, slice ham and pastry. Makes 16 to 18 servings. May be served hot or cold.

Meat is an excellent source of B-vitamins.

GLAZED HAM (HAM GLACÉ)

1 canned ham (5 pounds (2.25 kg),
   chilled
1 envelope unflavored gelatine
2 cans (10½ ounce (294 g) condensed
   beef consomme
4 tablespoons (60 ml) sherry wine

Thinly sliced stuffed olives
Pimiento
Thinly sliced green pepper
Tiny sprigs parsley

Remove ham from can. Combine gelatin from ham with unflavored gelatin and beef consomme in a saucepan. Stir over low heat until gelatin is melted. Add sherry. Scrape off any fat on ham and place ham on a cake rack set in a shallow pan.

Place pan of melted gelatin in a cold bath of water and ice cubes. Stir gently until gelatin begins to get sirupy. Pour some of sirupy gelatin carefully over ham. Chill. When gelatin is set on ham, spoon another layer of sirupy gelatin over ham Chill again. (If gelatin mixture gets too thick, heat until melted and chill again in ice bath.)

Decorate the ham as desired with olive slices, pimiento, green pepper and tiny sprigs of parsley, dipping pieces in the sirupy gelatin before arranging on ham. Chill and then add another coat of gelatin. Chill well. Gelatin that drips into the pan under the ham may be melted and reused if necessary.

To serve, place Glazed Ham on a platter and garnish as desired with parsley and slice into thin slices. Makes about 10 to 15 servings.

BAKED HAM WITH ORANGE SLICES AND BROWN SUGAR

One usually bakes a whole ham for a gala occasion. Make a big casserole of potatoes au gratin and combine green beans and sliced mushrooms to serve with the ham. Have Waldorf salad.

1 ham (cook before eating)
   (12 pounds − 5.40 kg)
1½ cups (375 ml) brown sugar

¾ cup (180 ml) water
3 or 4 cloves
2 to 3 navel oranges

Place ham on rack in roasting pan and bake at 325°F (160°C) for 1 − 1½ hours. Remove from oven and cut off skin from ham. Trim off as much fat as possible.

While ham is baking make sirup of brown sugar, water and cloves: Combine brown sugar with water and cloves and cook 5 minutes. Remove cloves.

Slice unpeeled oranges very thinly and place over ham. Secure with a piece of tooth pick if necessary. Pour sirup carefully over ham and oranges.

Return ham to oven and bake another 1½ hours (160°F-(70°C) on meat thermometer. Baste with pan juices.

Slice and serve. Makes 20 servings with leftovers.

ROAST LEG OF LAMB A LA SEVILLE

Serve parslied new potatoes and fried eggplant and mixed greens with lamb.

1 lamb leg (5 to 8 pounds)
    (2.25 to 3.6 kg)
Salt and fresh ground pepper
1 bay leaf, crushed
3 tablespoons (45 ml) butter or
    margarine

1 jar (4 ounce) (112 g) pimiento pieces,
    drained or 1 fresh pimiento, seeded
    and diced
¼ cup (50 ml) chopped parsley
1 cup (250 ml) dry white wine
1 clove garlic, chopped

Remove as much fat as possible from lamb and put on a rack in a roasting pan. Season with salt and pepper and press bay leaf onto lamb. Rub lamb with butter. Roast at 325°F (160°C) 30 minutes per pound or 160°F (70°C) on meat thermometer for medium doneness. Pour pan juices into a medium skillet. Saute garlic and pimiento in pan juices until garlic is tender. Add parsley and wine and heat. Serve sauce with sliced lamb. Makes 10 – 12 servings with leftovers.

CROWN ROAST OF LAMB

Something special for that Easter feast. Add oven browned potatoes if you feel the need.

1 Rack of lamb, about 3 pounds
    (1.35 kg)
1 teaspoon (5 ml) salt
Fresh ground pepper to taste
Paper frills
2 cups (500 ml) mixed peas and
    mushrooms, cooked

1 small head cauliflower, cooked
1 pound (0.45 kg) white pearl
    onions, cooked
Parsley
Mint sauce

Have meat man make rack of lamb into a crown roast. To roast, place upside down in a roasting pan. Season with salt and pepper. Insert a meat thermometer so the bulb reaches the thickest part of the meat, but does not touch bone. Roast at 325°F (160°C) 30 to 35 minutes per pound or about 2¼ hours. Medium done on the thermometer is 160°F (70°C).

To serve place rack bone side up on round platter. Put paper frills on bones. Fill center with peas and mushrooms and place cooked cauliflower in center of roast. Surround with onions and parsley. To carve, cut between ribs and serve vegetables with each chop. Pass mint sauce for individual service.

Mint Sauce: Combine 1 cup (250 ml) wine vinegar with ½ cup (125 ml) water and ½ cup (125 ml) sugar. Bring to a boil and pour over ½ cup (125 ml) firmly packed chopped fresh mint leaves. Steep for 1 to 2 minutes. Serve with lamb. Makes about 2 cups (500 ml).

ROAST VEAL WITH ROSEMARY

Oven bake tiny new potatoes to serve with butter or chopped parsley and, for a vegetable, peas with mushrooms.

5 pound (2.25 kg) rolled veal leg
1 teaspoon (5 ml) dried rosemary
1 clove garlic

1½ teaspoons (7.5 ml) salt
Fresh gound pepper to taste
3 slices bacon

Rub veal all over with rosemary, garlic, salt and pepper which have been mixed together in a mortar and pestle. Place on a rack in a shallow baking pan. Lay bacon strips over top of roast. Bake at 325°F (160°C) for 35 minutes per pound or about 3 hours. Baste occasionally with pan juices. Temperature on meat thermometer is 170°F (70°C). Makes 8 – 10 servings.

VEAL VIENNA

Serve knockerle or spaetzel and buttered beets with the veal.

2 pounds (0.9 kg) thinly sliced veal
    cut from leg
¼ cup (50 ml) flour
1 teaspoon (5 ml) salt
Fresh ground pepper to taste

4 tablespoons (60 ml) butter or
    margarine
1 large onion, sliced
1 tablespoon (15 ml) paprika
1 cup (250 ml) dairy sour cream

Pound veal slices with a mallet between pieces of wax paper until very thin. Mix flour with salt and pepper and dip veal slices in mixture.

Heat butter in skillet and fry the onion. Sprinkle with paprika. When onion begins to brown lightly, add floured veal and brown quickly on both sides. (Add additional butter if needed.) Transfer veal to platter as browned. When all veal is cooked, add sour cream to skillet and heat, do not boil. Serve with veal. Makes 6 servings.

Cook several days' dinner dishes on a single day.

40

THE BEST OF POT LUCK: POT ROAST, STEWS AND SOUPS

Certain pieces of meat are better when cooked with moist heat, or in liquid (braising or stewing). These are primarily the fore quarter and part of the leg (particularly in beef). The meat has higher muscle formation than the steak and roast section and needs the moisture to tenderize. It can be water, broth, juices, wine, milk, beer — any liquid which will make a tasty recipe.

All recipes that fall into this classification are almost better when reheated the second day because the flavors have a chance to blend, so they are good for plan-overs or work savers for the day of a party. I often make the meat and sauce part of a stew and then cook it with the required vegetables the day it is served. This gets some of the long cooking done the day before, but the vegetables are freshly cooked.

There is nothing better than homemade soup. It can be the basis for a simple supper. Or why not start a new custom with soup parties? A hearty homemade soup, lots of hot buttered French bread, cheese, fruit and wine is a feast fit for a king.

If you become a homemade soup fan you can also save money on your meat for stew purchases. Buy bone-in chuck roasts or steaks — cut out the bone and trim the suet (I freeze it for birds in the winter). The beef bones can be immediately made into soup or frozen for future use — the solid meat cut in stew cubes or larger for Swiss Steak.

Likewise both lamb and pork bones can be saved for soup making. Some of the tastiest soups I've made have been a combination of bones. Saving ham bones for soup and chicken or turkey carcasses are also worthwhile.

The recipes in this section take longer, slower cooking but are flavorful and nutritious.

My own cooking style is to follow directions carefully for roasts, steaks and chops. A too raw or a dried out roast or steak isn't very appetizing but with pot roasts, stews and soups let your imagination and likes take over. If garlic is not your thing, leave it out. If you prefer oregano instead of thyme use oregano. If you have tomato soup and no tomato sauce use it. Add a little wine to the liquid. Too many onions for you, cut down the amount.

So these recipes for pot roasts, soups and stews are the basic pattern. You can add your own embellishments to them after you've tried the original ones.

Most of the pot roast, etc., recipes in this section indicate top of the range cooking times. However, if you prefer, these dishes may be cooked in the oven at 300° to 325° F (145–160°C). The cooking container should be covered just as in top of the range cooking. When cooking in the oven, you will be conserving fuel to plan a meal around the meat, all of which can be cooked in the oven at the same time as the meat.

A pot roast can be anything from a boneless beef rolled rump (from the leg) to a beef arm or blade pot roast (from the chuck). Most of us choose the piece of meat which suits our needs the best. Here is how I make my basic pot roast.

4 to 5 pounds (1.8 to 2.25 kg) beef pot roast	1 cup (250 ml) water
1 teaspoon (5 ml) salt	1 bouillon cube
Freshly ground pepper to taste	3 tablespoons (45 ml) flour
1 large onion, coarsely cut	

Use a Dutch oven with a tight fitting lid or a large skillet with a dome cover (aluminum or iron is best). An electric skillet with a dome lid or deep sides is excellent. Rub the meat with salt and pepper. Over moderately high heat brown the meat nicely on all surfaces. Then pour off all the accumulated fat from the skillet. Put in the onion pieces and cook them until nicely browned. Reduce the heat, add the water and bouillon cube. When the liquid comes to a boil, cover the container and keep the heat low enough so the liquid barely simmers. At the end of the first hour turn the meat over and, if needed, add a little more water. A flat arm or blade pot roast will take from 2½ to 3½ hours to cook. A thicker piece of meat such as a boneless rolled rump roast may take a little longer since the heat is slower penetrating the center of the meat. If you like, about ¾ of an hour before the meat is done, enough peeled potatoes to serve the required number of people may be added. Also carrots, peeled and cut in sizable chunks.

When the pot roast is done remove from pan to a platter and keep warm. Also remove potatoes and carrots if any.

Skim off as much fat as possible and measure liquid. Add water to make 2 cups (500 ml). Return to pan. If you have a whisk the flour can be whisked into the liquid and it will not lump. If you don't, mix a little additional water with the flour to make a thin paste and add that to the liquid in the pan stirring briskly as you add it. Taste and see if it needs additional salt. Or you might want to add some Worcestershire or thick steak sauce. If you like the gravy a little more brown, add a bit of gravy browner. At any rate, cook and stir the gravy until it boils and is thickened. Slice the pot roast and serve with potatoes and gravy. A 4 to 5 pound (1.8 to 2.25 kg) pot roast should serve 6 to 8 with meat left over.

VARIATIONS

Mushroom Pot Roast

Wash and slice 4 ounces (112 gm) fresh mushrooms or use 1 can (6-ounce— 168 gm) sliced mushrooms.

Saute fresh mushrooms with onion, before adding to pot roast or, add canned mushrooms (including liquid) to pot roast when ready to simmer. Add also 1 teaspoon (5 ml) Worcestershire sauce.

Barbecued Pot Roast

Omit water and use instead 1 cup (250 ml) of your favorite barbecue sauce. If additional liquid is needed during cooking, add water. Do not make gravy. Skim off as much of the fat as possible and serve sauce with meat.

Tomato Pot Roast

Omit water and use instead 1 cup (250 ml) tomato juice. If additional liquid is needed during cooking add tomato juice. To make gravy, add water to pan juices to make 2 cups (500 ml). In addition to tomato juice, add ½ teaspoon (2 ml) each celery and garlic salt, dried oregano and basil.

Wine Pot Roast

Omit Water and use 1 can (8-ounce – 224 gm) tomato sauce and 1 cup (250 ml) dry red wine. Add ½ teaspoon (2 ml) each marjoram, thyme and basil. If desired add 1 clove garlic, finely minced.

POT ROAST IN FOIL

Another method of pot roasting which appeals to many people is to wrap the meat in aluminum foil and cook it in the oven. Here is how it is done.

4 – 5 pound (1.8 – 2.25 kg)
   boneless beef pot roast
1 teaspoon (5 ml) salt
Freshly ground pepper to taste
1 medium onion, diced
1 carrot, peeled and diced

1 small stalk of celery, diced
1 bay leaf
½ teaspoon (2 ml) thyme
Few sprigs parsley

Measure a length of heavy duty foil long enough to completely wrap pot roast and vegetables. Place foil in a shallow pan and place pot roast in center. Fold foil up and around meat and broil meat, turning to brown all surfaces. Remove from broiler and season with salt and pepper. Add vegetables, bay leaf, thyme and parsley. Close foil, sealing edges with a tight, double fold to form an airtight package.

Place in oven (in pan) and bake at 300°F (150°C) 3 to 3½ hours. Or bake at 250°F (120°C) 4½ hours. When roast is done open foil and remove meat to a platter. Pour the meat juices and vegetables into a saucepan and skim off fat. Taste for seasoning. Serve with pot roast. Makes 8 – 10 servings.

SPECIAL POT ROAST

3 to 4 pound (1.35 to 1.8 kg)
   rolled rump roast
1 piece of Polish (Kielbasa)
   sausage, length of roast

Salt and fresh ground pepper
1 cup (250 ml) bouillon

Either have the meat man tie rump roast around a piece of Polish (Kielbasa) sausage (skinned) or take the roast apart and do it yourself and retie the roast with string. Rub in salt and pepper. Brown on all surfaces over moderately high heat in a Dutch oven or a domed skillet. Pour off fat. Add bouillon and cook meat 3½−4 hours or until tender. Slice finished pot roast so each slice has a piece of sausage. Remove as much fat as possible from pan juices and serve with roast. Makes 8 servings with leftovers.

SWISS STEAK

Swiss Steak was one of the earliest "foreign" recipes to come to this country and particularly in the middle west where recipes for Swiss Steak have been handed down for several generations. It has multiple variations — is a good keeper if dinner is delayed and when you are not sure how a piece of round steak will react to pan broiling, Swiss Steak will always be tender and flavorful. The old fashioned way — to pound flour into the meat with the edge of a saucer (my grandmother had a heavy edged saucer special for this purpose) is still the best, though you may use a mallet or meat hammer. Boiled potatoes and diced carrots are good served with it.

3 pounds (1.35 kg) round steak or
   chuck arm steak about
   1-inch (2.5 cm) thick
¼ cup (50 ml) flour
1 teaspoon (5 ml) salt

Fresh ground pepper to taste
2 tablespoons (30 ml) butter
   or margarine
1 large onion, sliced
1 cup (250 ml) water

Trim fat from meat and remove bones if any. Cut into serving pieces. Place on a piece of wax paper.

Mix flour with salt and pepper. Using the edge of a heavy saucer, pound flour mixture into meat turning and pounding flour into both sides.

Heat butter in skillet and brown meat quickly on both sides. Add onion and water, reduce heat, and cover with a tight lid. Cook on low heat so meat just simmers until tender, about 2−2½ hours. If necessary more liquid can be added during cooking. Serve meat with gravy. Makes 6 servings.

Mushroom Swiss Steak

Cut 2 slices bacon in pieces. Fry in a large skillet until crisp. Push to one side and brown prepared steak in bacon fat. Add 1 medium onion, chopped and brown onion. Add 1 can 10½ ounce – 294 g) cream of mushroom soup instead of water and ½ teaspoon (2 ml) each nutmeg and sage. Bring to a boil and simmer, covered, 2–2½ hours until meat is tender. Serve with gravy.

Tomato Swiss Steak

Brown prepared meat as directed. Omit water and add 1½ cups (375 ml) canned tomatoes, ¼ teaspoon (1 ml) cloves, ½ teaspoon (2 ml) chili powder, 2 tablespoons (30 ml) each chopped parsley, chopped green pepper. Bring to a boil and simmer, covered, 2–2½ hours or until tender.

Wine Swiss Steak

Brown prepared meat as directed. Add 1 clove garlic, cut up, 1 teaspoon (5 ml) rosemary. Omit water and add 1 cup (250 ml) dry red wine (Chianti or Burgundy). Bring to a boil and simmer, covered, 2–2½ hours or until tender.

Swiss Steak with Sour Cream

Brown prepared meat as directed. Add 1 cup (250 ml) sliced mushrooms and saute for several minutes. Add water and 1 teaspoon (5 ml) Worcestershire sauce. Bring to a boil and simmer, covered, 2–2½ hours until tender. Remove meat from pan and stir in ½ cup (125 ml) dairy sour cream. Heat but do not boil.

Swiss Steak and Vegetables

Brown prepared meat as directed. Add 2 carrots, sliced, 2 stalks celery, diced and use an additional sliced onion. Omit water and add 1 can (8-ounce (224 gm) tomato sauce and ½ bay leaf. Bring to a boil and simmer, covered, 2–2½ hours or until tender.

BRISKET OF BEEF WITH BEANS

A very good combination and one that takes little watching during cooking. Start the meal with chilled tomato juice and serve cole slaw with the brisket.

1 pound (0.45 kg) dried navy beans
3 to 4 pound (1.35 – 1.80 kg)
    brisket of beef
½ teaspoon (2 ml) dry mustard
½ cup (125 ml) light brown sugar

½ cup (125 ml) maple sirup
2 teaspoons (10 ml) salt
Fresh ground pepper to taste

Pick over and wash beans. Soak overnight in water to cover. Trim fat from brisket. Put beans and liquid in a large casserole. Stir in mustard, sugar, sirup and salt. Place brisket of beef on top of beans and add enough additional water to cover meat. Cover casserole and bake at 350°F (175°C) until meat is tender and beans are done, about 3 hours. Add additional water as needed. Makes 6 servings.

OXTAIL RAGOUT

A good oxtail ragout is delicious fare. Allow enough time for the meat on the oxtails to become tender. In fact this is one dish that can readily be prepared the day before and reheated. With it serve a simple lettuce salad, French bread.

2 oxtails (about 2½ pounds
    (1.25 kg), cut in 2-inch
    (5 cm) lengths
2 tablespoons (30 ml) butter
    or margarine
1 clove garlic, finely diced
4 medium onions, sliced
2 cups (500 ml) beef bouillon

2 cups (500 ml) canned tomatoes
½ cup (125 ml) dry red wine
1 teaspoon (5 ml) salt
Fresh ground pepper to taste
4 medium potatoes, peeled

Wipe oxtails with a damp towel and trim off as much fat as possible. Brown oxtails in butter on all sides. Add garlic and onions and brown lightly. Add bouillon, tomatoes, wine, salt and pepper and simmer 3 hours or until meat is tender. Add potatoes and cook another 30 minutes. Skim off as much fat as possible. Makes 4 servings.

BEEF STEW ROMANO

Serve Beef Stew Romano with spaghetti and a large tossed salad. Be sure to include Italian or French bread.

2 lbs. (0.9 kg) boneless beef
   for stew
1 teaspoon (5 ml) salt
Fresh ground pepper to taste
3 tablespoons (45 ml) flour
2 tablespoons (30 ml) oil
1 clove garlic, finely diced

1 large onion, chopped
¼ teaspoon (1 ml) dried oregano
¼ teaspoon (1 ml) dried basil
⅛ teaspoon (0.5 ml) ground cloves
1 can (16 ounce – 448 gm) tomato sauce
1 cup (250 ml) water

Sprinkle beef with salt, pepper and flour. Heat oil in heavy skillet and brown beef, garlic and onions over moderate heat. Add remaining ingredients. Bring to a boil and simmer, covered, 2 hours or until beef is tender. Makes 4 to 6 servings.

BEEF A LA MODE

Traditionally the beef for beef a la mode is larded. Perhaps you can get your meat man to do it for you. If not, and you do not have a larding needle to do it yourself, go ahead and make the recipe. It will still be good. There are vegetables in the recipe — add boiled potatoes and a cranberry relish to serve with it.

4 – 5 pound (1.8 – 2.25 kg)
   piece of beef round or chuck
¼ cup (50 ml) flour
1 teaspoon (5 ml) salt
Fresh ground pepper to taste
¼ cup (50 ml) chopped suet
2 cups (500 ml) beef stock or bouillon

1 medium onion, sliced
1 cup (250 ml) julienne carrots
1½ cups (375 ml) diced white turnips
1½ cups (375 ml) peas
½ cup (125 ml) dry red wine

Rub meat with flour, salt and pepper. Heat suet in a Dutch oven or domed skillet and brown meat on all surfaces. Add 1 cup (250 ml) of the stock and the onions and simmer, covered, for about 3 hours or until meat is tender. Add additional stock if needed during cooking.

Add vegetables about 30 minutes before meat is done.

To serve: Remove meat and let stand 15 minutes. Remove all fat possible from liquid in pan. Measure and add wine and enough additional stock to make 2 cups (500 ml). Mix 3 tablespoons (45 ml) flour with enough water to make a thin paste and stir into stock-wine mixture. Taste and correct seasonings. Cook and stir until mixture boils and is thickened. Slice meat and arrange slices down center of large platter. Surround with vegetables. Serve with gravy. Makes 8 to 10 servings.

BEEF AND MUSHROOM RAGOUT

A casserole of hot noodles and fresh vegetable relishes go well with this dish.

3 pounds (1.35 kg) boneless beef chuck
2 cups (500 ml) sliced onions
2 tablespoons (30 ml) bacon fat
1½ tablespoons (25 ml) flour
1½ teaspoons (7.5 ml) salt
Fresh ground pepper to taste

½ teaspoon (2 ml) dried marjoram
½ teaspoon (2 ml) dried oregano
½ cup (125 ml) beef bouillon
1 cup (250 ml) dry red wine
½ pound (0.225 kg) fresh
   mushrooms, sliced

Cut beef chuck into 1½ inch (3.75 cm) cubes. Saute onion in bacon fat in a large skillet until lightly browned. Remove and reserve. Add beef to skillet and brown on all sides. Sprinkle with flour and add seasonings. Add bouillon and wine. Bring to a boil, cover and simmer over low heat for 2 hours, adding additional wine as needed to keep meat barely covered. Add cooked onions and mushrooms and continue cooking until meat is tender, 30 to 40 minutes. Makes 6 servings.

BEEF CARBONNADE

Beef Carbonnade is of Belgian origin — the beef is cooked in a sauce, the main ingredient of which is beer. It is traditionally served with boiled potatoes. For a vegetable serve broccoli and make a salad of sliced oranges and onions on lettuce.

1 pint (500 ml) beer
2 pounds (0.9 kg) beef for
   stew, cubed
3 tablespoons (45 ml) flour
1 teaspoon (5 ml) salt

Fresh ground pepper to taste
1 medium onion, sliced
2 tablespoons (30 ml) butter
   or margarine
½ teaspoon (2 ml) sugar

Open beer and let stand to get flat. Mix beef with flour, salt and pepper. Fry with onion in butter in a large skillet until browned. Add beer and sugar. Simmer, covered, about 2 hours or until tender. Makes 4 to 6 servings.

Meat has a high satiety value, keeps you from getting hungry longer.

48

Braising of pork chops used to be about the only way they were cooked. The wonderful flavor of fork tender pork with a delicious sauce is hard to beat.

6 pork chops (1-inch — 2.5 cm) thick   Freshly ground pepper to taste
3 tablespoons (45 ml) flour   ½ cup (125 ml) water or bouillon
1 teaspoon (5 ml) salt

Trim off fat from pork chops and heat fat slowly in large skillet to use for browning chops. Mix flour with salt and pepper and coat chops on both sides in flour mixture. Brown in skillet, turning to brown both sides, over moderately high heat. Add water and simmer, covered tightly, about 1 hour or until tender. If needed, add additional water during cooking. Serve pork chops with liquid from skillet. Makes 6 servings.

VARIATIONS

Chili Chops

After browning, add ½ cup (125 ml) water and ½ cup (125 ml) chili sauce and 1 teaspoon (5 ml) Worcestershire sauce. Simmer, covered, until tender. Serve chops with sauce.

Provincial

Saute 1 medium onion chopped in skillet while browning pork chops. Add 1 cup (250 ml) tomato sauce and 1 teaspoon (5 ml) each of oregano and basil. Simmer, covered, until tender.

Rosemary

After browning, add ½ cup (125 ml) dry white wine and 1 teaspoon (5 ml) crushed dried rosemary. Simmer, covered, until tender. Add additional wine during cooking if needed.

Country Style

After browning, add 1 cup (250 ml) half and half milk. Simmer covered, until tender. Mix 1 tablespoon (15 ml) flour with enough water to make a thin paste. Add to liquid in pan, stirring briskly. Bring to a boil. Add seasoning as needed. Serve with chops.

With Sauerkraut

After browning, add ½ cup (125 ml) apple juice, 1 small onion, chopped, and 2 cups (500 ml) drained sauerkraut. Simmer covered, until tender.

PORK WITH SAUERKRAUT

This pork stew is a delightful combination of flavors. A baked potato would go well with it and some corn muffins.

2 pounds (0.9 kg) boned pork, cubed
1 large onion, diced
1 clove garlic, diced, optional
1 tablespoon (15 ml) bacon fat
1 tablespoon (15 ml) chopped parsley
½ teaspoon (2 ml) dried sage

1 cup (250 ml) water
1 beef bouillon cube
½ teaspoon (2 ml) caraway seeds
1 can (20 ounce – 560 gm) sauerkraut
1 apple peeled and diced
1 tablespoon (15 ml) brown sugar

Brown pork, onion and garlic in bacon fat in a Dutch oven. Add remaining ingredients and simmer, covered, about 1 to 1½ hours or until tender. Makes 4 to 6 servings.

PORK CHOP RICE CASSEROLE

Take advantage of the oven and bake a dish of carrots to serve with the casserole. A pineapple and grape dessert salad finishes the meal.

4 loin pork chops, about 1-inch
    (2.5 cm) thick
½ cup (125 ml) long cooking rice
1 can (1 pound – 228 gm) tomatoes
1 cup (250 ml) tomato juice
1 teaspoon (5 ml) sugar

1½ teaspoons (7.5 ml) salt
½ cup (125 ml) minced onion
½ teaspoon (2 ml) dried marjoram
½ teaspoon (2 ml) dried rosemary
1 medium bay leaf

Brown pork chops on both sides in skillet. Remove from skillet, add rice and cook and stir until lightly browned. Spoon rice into a buttered 6-cup (1.44 L) flat casserole. Arrange pork chops on top of rice. Add remaining ingredients to skillet and heat. Pour over pork chops in casserole. Bake, covered, at 350°F (175°C) oven for 45 minutes. Uncover, bake 15 minutes longer. Makes 4 servings.

BRAISED VEAL STEAK

Veal is delicately flavored and in cooking reacts with more grace to subtle seasonings. The veal arm steak is cut from the arm roast, a part of the forequarter or shoulder. This cut can also be made into veal cutlets by boning and slicing the meat very thin. A veal arm steak cut about an inch thick will usually weigh about 2 pounds (0.90 kg) and serve 4.

1 veal arm steak, ¾ – 1 inch
  (1.88 – 2.5 cm) thick
2 tablespoons (30 ml) butter
  or margarine

Fresh ground pepper to taste
1 cup (250 ml) bouillon
¾ teaspoon (3.75 ml) salt

Trim fat from steak. Heat butter in a skillet with a tight lid. Brown veal on both sides. Add remaining ingredients. Cover and simmer 45 to 50 minutes or until tender. Makes 3 to 4 servings.

VARIATIONS

Veal and Mushrooms

To browned veal add 2 tablespoons (30 ml) chopped onion, 1 small can (4 ounce – 112 gm) mushrooms and liquid, 2 tablespoons (30 ml) chopped parsley. Simmer, covered, until tender.

Veal with Sour Cream

To browned veal steak add ¼ cup (50 ml) water, 1 teaspoon (5 ml) paprika, ½ teaspoon (2 ml) nutmeg. Simmer, covered, until tender. Remove veal from pan and keep warm. Add ½ cup (125 ml) sour cream to gravy in pan and heat, do not boil. Serve with veal.

Herbed Veal

To browned veal add ½ teaspoon (2 ml) each of dried rosemary, basil and thyme, 1 cup (250 ml) dry white wine. Cover and simmer, letting liquid evaporate so that veal is served without sauce. Dust with finely chopped parsley.

Curried Veal

To browned veal add 1 to 2 teaspoons (5 to 10 ml) curry powder, ½ cup (125 ml) apple sauce, 1 tablespoon (15 ml) grated onion, 1 cup (250 ml) chicken broth. Cover and simmer until tender.

Tomato Veal

To browned veal add 1 clove chopped garlic, 1 teaspoon (5 ml) basil, 3 tablespoons (45 ml) tomato paste and 1 cup (250 ml) dry white wine. Cover and simmer until tender.

BAKED VEAL STEW SUPREME

The creamy gravy would go nicely with rice. For the rest of the menu serve sauted celery and carrot slaw.

2 tablespoons (30 ml) flour
1 teaspoon (5 ml) salt
½ teaspoon (2 ml) paprika
½ teaspoon (2 ml) poultry dressing
Fresh ground pepper
1½ pounds (0.675 kg) boneless veal, cubed

4 tablespoons (60 ml) butter or margarine
½ cup (125 ml) water
1 can (10¾ ounce – 301 g) condensed cream of chicken soup
1 cup (250 ml) soft bread crumbs
¼ cup (50 ml) Parmesan cheese

Mix flour with seasonings and coat veal cubes with mixture. Heat 2 tablespoons (30 ml) butter in a skillet and brown veal. Put veal into buttered casserole. Add water and soup to skillet and heat and scrape and stir crust from bottom. Pour over veal in casserole. Melt remaining butter and mix with crumbs and cheese and sprinkle over veal in casserole. Bake at 350°F (175°C) 45 to 50 minutes or until meat is tender. Makes 4 to 5 servings.

OSSO BUCO

A famous Italian dish made with veal shank. Serve rice with the tasty gravy and a vegetable, perhaps buttered peas.

3 veal shanks, each cut in 2-inch (5 cm) thick pieces
5 tablespoons (75 ml) flour
1 teaspoon (5 ml) salt
Freshly ground pepper to taste
2 tablespoons (30 ml) butter or margarine
2 tablespoons (30 ml) olive oil
3 tomatoes, peeled and chopped
1 large onion, chopped

2 cloves garlic, pressed
½ teaspoon (2 ml) dried thyme
½ teaspoon (2 ml) dried rosemary
1 carrot, diced
1 stalk celery, diced
1½ cups (375 ml) dry white wine
1 cup (250 ml) chicken broth
Juice of one lemon
2 tablespoons (30 ml) chopped parlsey

Roll veal shanks in flour seasoned with salt and pepper. Heat butter and olive oil in a large Dutch oven and brown veal shanks on all sides. Arrange veal shanks on side, then add remaining ingredients except lemon and parsley. Bring to a boil, cover and simmer until veal is tender, about 2 hours. When veal is done sprinkle with lemon juice and parsley just before serving. Makes 6 to 8 servings.

VEAL SCALLOPINI MILAN

With the veal and green noodles serve an escarole salad.

2½ pounds (1.125 kg) veal for
   scallopini
¼ cup (50 ml) flour
4 tablespoons (60 ml) oil
3 cloves garlic, chopped
4 small onions, chopped
2 cups (500 ml) bouillon

1 cup (250 ml) dry white wine
2 cups (500 ml) tomato juice
1 teaspoon (5 ml) dried rosemary
1½ teaspoon (7.5 ml) salt
Fresh ground pepper to taste
3 tablespoons (45 ml) chopped parsley
1 pound (448 gm) green noodles

Pound veal very thin. Dredge lightly with flour. Brown lightly in oil on both sides, adding more oil if necessary. Remove veal from pan as browned. Brown garlic and onion in same pan. Add bouillon, wine and tomato juice to pan and return meat to pan. Sprinkle with rosemary, salt and pepper. Cover and simmer one hour or until tender. Serve on a hot platter surrounded by green noodles, cooked as directed on package. Sprinkle with chopped parsley. Makes 6 servings.

VEAL AMERICAN

Vermicelli and lightly sauteed zucchini with a crisp lettuce salad can complete the menu.

3 tablespoons (45 ml) oil
1 clove garlic, cut in half
1½ pounds (0.675 kg) thin sliced
   veal cutlet
3 tablespoons (45 ml) flour
½ teaspoon (2 ml) salt
Fresh ground pepper to taste

⅛ teaspoon (0.5 ml) paprika
1 can (4 ounce − 112 gm) sliced
   mushrooms and liquid
1 cup (250 ml) beef bouillon
1 tablespoon (15 ml) chopped parsley
1 teaspoon (5 ml) vinegar
Grated Parmesan cheese

Heat oil in skillet with garlic over low heat. Pound veal with mallet until very thin. Mix flour with salt, pepper and paprika and dip veal slices in mixture. Remove garlic from oil and discard. Increase heat to moderately high and brown veal. When all veal is browned, add mushrooms and liquid and bouillon. Cover and simmer 25 to 30 minutes or until tender. Stir in parsley and vinegar and serve with Parmesan cheese. Makes 4 servings.

PERSIAN LAMB

This is a little different from the ordinary "stew" but good. Serve green beans and sliced tomato salad with it.

2 onions, sliced
2 tablespoons (30 ml) butter or
    margarine
2 pounds (0.90 kg) boneless diced lamb
2 cups (500 ml) bouillon
1 teaspoon (5 ml) salt

Fresh ground pepper
1 cup (250 ml) long cooking rice
1 package (10 ounce — 220 gm) frozen
    lima beans, defrosted
2 tablespoons (30 ml) dried dill weed
2 tablespoons (30 ml) chopped parsley

Saute onions in butter until lightly browned. Remove from skillet to a saucepan and brown the lamb, adding additional butter if needed. Heat bouillon in skillet, scraping to remove all the browned crust. Add to onions and lamb in saucepan Add salt and pepper to taste. Bring to a boil and simmer, covered, for about one hour.

Mix rice with lima beans, dill weed and chopped parsley. Put one-third the rice in a buttered 2-quart (1.90 L) casserole. Add a layer of meat and onions. Add one-third rice mixture. Add remaining meat and top with remaining rice. Pour liquid in which meat was cooked over all. Cover and bake at 350°F (175°C) for 40 to 50 minutes or until rice is fluffy and tender. Add additional bouillon to casserole, if needed, during cooking. Makes 6 servings.

LAMB STEW WITH DUMPLINGS

2 tablespoons (30 ml) butter or
    margarine
3 pounds (1.35 kg) boneless lamb diced
1 teaspoon (5 ml) salt
Fresh ground pepper to taste
2 onions, sliced

½ teaspoon (2 ml) dried thyme
3 cups (750 ml) boiling water
¾ pound (0.34 kg) string beans
4 – 5 medium carrots
Parsley dumplings

Heat butter in a heavy Dutch oven and brown lamb on all surfaces. Add salt, pepper, onions, thyme and boiling water. Cover and simmer about 1 hour or until lamb is just tender. Wash, trim and cut beans into 1-inch pieces and peel and cut carrots in half. Add to lamb and cook another 20 minutes, covered. Put dumplings on top of stew by tablespoons and cook over low heat uncovered 10 minutes and covered 10 minutes. Makes 6 servings.

Parsley Dumplings

2 cups (500 ml) buttermilk baking mix
⅔ cup (150 ml) milk

4 tablespoons (60 ml) chopped parsley

Lightly mix all ingredients with a fork. Spoon dough onto boiling stew.

54

BEEF VEGETABLE SOUP

It is easier to make soup a two day preparation. If the beef stock is cooked the first day, it can be cooled, the meat removed from the bone and diced, the stock refrigerated so any fat is easily taken off. Then the vegetables added and cooked the next day. This hearty soup is great for lunch with a sandwich.

3 to 4 pound (1.35 – 1.8 kg) soup
   bone with meat
2 quarts (1.90 L) cold water
1 onion
1 teaspoon (5 ml) salt
6 whole peppercorns

6 sprigs parsley, snipped
¼ cup (50 ml) rice or barley
4 carrots
2 cups (500 ml) diced potatoes
1 cup (250 ml) chopped celery
2 cups (500 ml) canned tomatoes

To make beef stock: In a large saucepan combine soup bone, meat, water, onion, salt and pepper. Bring to a boil and skim off foam. Cook, covered, over low heat 2 to 3 hours or until meat is tender. Cool. Remove meat from bone and dice. (Discard bone). Strain. Skim fat from stock. Add meat and remaining ingredients to stock and cook, covered, over low heat 30 minutes. This makes about 3 quarts (2.85 L) soup.

Note #1: If barley is used, soak overnight in water to cover.
Note #2: If beef stock is to be used for onion or mushroom soup, use meat to make sandwich spread or hash or freeze for future use.

ONION SOUP

The beef stock which is made in the vegetable soup can be the basis for other interesting soups, of which onion soup is one. Onion soup gained its initial fame in Les Halles, the famous French market in Paris where everyone went to eat it after parties, and met workmen who were enjoying it before starting work.

A bowl of onion soup and a tossed green salad with fruit for dessert is a good meal.

Prepare beef stock as directed.

4 tablespoons (60 ml) butter or
   margarine
2 cups (500 ml) sliced Bermuda onions
6 cups (1.44 L) beef stock

Salt, fresh ground pepper to taste
6 slices French bread
Grated Parmesan cheese

Heat butter in a good sized saucepan. Add onions and saute slowly until tender but not browned. They should still have a slight firmness. Add beef stock and heat to boiling. Season to taste with salt and pepper. Spoon soup into 6 oven proof marmite or soup dishes. Toast French bread slices — place one in each soup dish and sprinkle generously with Parmesan cheese. Run under the broiler until cheese is melted. Makes 6 servings.

Note: If the onions are sliced on the bias so the rings are not whole, onion soup is easier to eat.

Prepare beef stock as directed.

¼ pound (112 gm) salt pork, diced
1 large onion, diced
1 cup (250 ml) peeled or diced Hubbard
    or other hard shelled squash

1 cup (250 ml) peeled and diced sweet
    potatoes
1 cup (250 ml) peeled and diced white
    potatoes
1 cup (250 ml) canned chick peas,
    drained
½ cup (125 ml) uncooked macaroni

Brown pork in skillet. Remove pork and cook onion until tender. Add pork, onion, squash, potatoes and chick peas to stock and simmer, covered, about 1 hour. Add macaroni and diced meat (from beef stock) and cook 20 to 30 minutes longer. Makes about 2½ quarts (2.375 L).

OTHER VARIATIONS

Mushroom Soup

Prepare beef stock as directed.

Slice ½ pound (224 gm) fresh mushrooms and saute in 2 tablespoons (30 ml) butter or margarine until lightly browned. Stir in 3 tablespoons (45 ml) flour, ¼ teaspoon (1 ml) nutmeg, ¼ teaspoon (1 ml) dried rosemary and 1 quart (.95 L) beef stock. Cook and stir until mixture boils and is thickened. Season to taste with salt and pepper. Makes 6 cups (1.5 L).

Leek Soup

Prepare beef stock as directed.

Clean 3 leeks well and cut into thin slices. Saute in 3 tablespoons (45 ml) butter or margarine until tender and lightly browned. Add 1 quart (.95 L) beef stock, a bouquet garni made of ¼ teaspoon (1 ml) dried thyme, 1 bay leaf, 3 cloves and 2 sprigs parsley tied in a cheesecloth bag, and 1½ cups (375 ml) diced potatoes. Simmer for 30 minutes. Remove bouquet garni and stir in ½ cup (125 ml) light cream. Season to taste with salt and pepper. Makes about 6 cups (1.5 L).

Always use the liquids in which meat is cooked, as a base for soups or a sauce to go with the meat cooked in it.

SAUSAGE — KALE SOUP

Lots of crusty bread and a cheese tray will complement this soup.

1 cup (250 ml) dried pea beans
1 large onion, sliced
½ pound (0.225 kg) pepperoni or
   Keilbasa sausage

1 pound (0.45 kg) kale
2 teaspoons (10 ml) salt
2½ quarts (2.375 L) water
2 cups (500 ml) cubed potatoes

Wash and pick over beans. Soak over night in water to cover. Next morning put in a large saucepan. Add onion. Remove skin from sausage, if any, and slice crosswise into thin slices. Wash kale well and chop in small pieces. Add sausage, kale, salt and water to beans and onions. Bring to a boil and cook until beans are tender, about 2½ hours. Add potatoes and cook 30 minutes longer. Add additional water if necessary. Makes about 3 quarts (2.85 L).

MINESTRONE

An Italian soup that is a meal, so thick is it with vegetables and bacon. Italian bread and cheese and fresh fruit can complete the meal.

1 cup (250 ml) dried navy beans
¼ pound (112 gm) fat salt pork
1 clove garlic, diced
1 onion, thinly sliced
½ pound (224 gm) bacon
2 large potatoes, peeled and diced
2 large carrots, peeled and diced
3 stalks celery, sliced
2 medium zucchini, sliced

1 cup (250 ml) canned tomatoes
3 quarts (2.85 L) water
2 cups (500 ml) shredded cabbage
1 package (10 ounce – 280 gm)
   frozen peas
½ cup (125 ml) long cooking rice*
¼ cup (50 ml) snipped parsley
Salt and fresh ground pepper to taste
Grated Parmesan cheese

Pick over and wash beans well. Soak overnight in water to cover. The next morning cook about 1 hour or until partially done.

Meanwhile, dice salt pork and fry in large Dutch oven or saucepan with garlic and onion until lightly browned. Cut bacon slices in thin strips crosswise. Add bacon, beans with liquid in which cooked, potatoes, carrots, celery, zucchini and tomatoes to the pan and add the water. Bring to a boil and simmer, covered, for about 1½ hours. Add cabbage, peas, rice and parsley and cook for another 30 minutes. Season to taste with salt and pepper. To serve sprinkle each bowl generously with grated Parmesan cheese. Makes about 3½ quarts (3.3 L).

* 1 cup (250 ml) uncooked elbow macaroni can be used in place of rice.

SPLIT PEA AND LENTIL SOUP

This recipe is a energy saver and a way to have a flavorful soup and a meat course from one pot. Serve a cup of this soup as a first course, then the pork with boiled cabbage and carrots. Chilled apple sauce may be an accompaniment or a dessert.

¾ cup (180 ml) green split peas
¾ cup (180 ml) lentils
1 medium onion, sliced

2½ quarts (2.38 L) water
2 pounds (0.90 kg) smoked pork
   shoulder roll

Pick over and wash peas and lentils. Combine with onion and water in a large saucepan. Bring to a boil and simmer about 1 hour. Add smoked shoulder roll and simmer an additional hour or until shoulder roll and peas and lentils are cooked. Remove shoulder roll and slice to serve. Serve pea mixture as soup. Makes about 6 servings of meat and soup.

SPLIT PEA SOUP

When split pea soup is made with a ham bone the flavor and heartiness of the soup makes it a perennial favorite. Split pea soup served with thick slices of homemade rye bread and butter, sliced tomatoes and cake with ice cream is a good lunch or supper.

Ham bone from baked ham (or fresh
   pork)
2½ quarts (2.38 L) water
1 whole onion
6 whole peppercorns

1 pound (0.45 kg) green split peas
1 large carrot, peeled and finely
   diced
1 onion, finely chopped
1 teaspoon (5 ml) celery salt

To make stock: Cook ham bone with water, whole onion and peppercorns for 2 hours, covered. Strain and remove meat from bone and dice. Pick over and wash peas well. Measure stock and, if needed, add water to make 2½ quarts (2.38 L). Combine in a large kettle, stock, diced ham, peas, carrots, chopped onion and celery salt. Simmer 2 hours or until peas are tender, stirring occasionally. Taste and add additional seasoning if necessary. Makes about 2 quarts (1.9 L).

VARIATION: Serve soup with thinly sliced frankfurters.

When you have roast lamb, save the bone (with a little meat on it) for Mulligatawney Soup. This dish, lightly flavored with curry, is a hearty soup which with crackers and a dessert such as Apple Dumplings can make a meal. Mulligatawney is also a recipe that can be a 2 day preparation. (If you don't have left-over lamb bones, buy some breast or other inexpensive cut).

2 – 3 pounds (0.9 – 1.35 kg) lamb
  bones with meat
1 carrot, peeled
1 piece celery
6 whole peppercorns
1 teaspoon (5 ml) salt
2 quarts (1.9 L) water

2 tablespoons (30 ml) butter or
  margarine
1 large onion chopped
2 leeks, sliced thin (or use
  green onions)
2 apples, peeled and diced
1½ teaspoons (7.5 ml) curry powder
¼ cup (50 ml) rice

Combine lamb bones and meat with carrot, celery, peppercorns, salt and water in a large saucepan. Bring to a boil and skim. Cover and simmer 2 hours. Cool. Remove bone and cut off and dice meat and reserve. Strain stock.

Heat butter and saute onion, leeks and apples until tender but not browned. Add curry powder, rice, lamb stock and meat. Bring to a boil and simmer, covered, for 30 minutes. Makes about 3 quarts soup.

Heat only enough water to make a cup of tea or coffee rather than the whole teakettle full.

NONE-OF-THE-OLD-GRIND
GROUND MEAT RECIPES

Often we think only of beef when ground meat is mentioned, but ground fresh pork is quite regularly on sale at the meat counter — ground lamb and veal occasionally. Most markets I know will special grind meat on request.

If you have a meat grinder or one of the new food processing machines you can grind your own. It does have a different texture than commercially ground meat and has the advantage of your knowing exactly what is in it. Very often the "bargain" beef chuck pot roasts that were mentioned in the stew chapter end up in home ground beef.

BASIC MEAT LOAF

Many discussions revolve around meat loaf since almost everyone has their favorite recipe. The basic meat loaf given here is one which I have made for many years. Whenever ground beef is on special, I make a meat loaf double-size and freeze part. It makes good sandwiches for lunch or lunch box. To freeze, the cooked loaf may be sliced into thin slices after it has cooled and the slices frozen with a piece of foil or plastic wrap between each. Put the packaged slices in a freezer bag and freeze. By doing it this way you can take out any number of slices at a time and reseal the bag. I suggest grated onion because you get the onion flavor without the pieces of onion. Always plan dinner around the oven when baking meat loaf — put it potatoes and a casserole of broccoli to bake at the same time.

3 medium slices bread, cubed or
  ½ cup (125 ml) dry bread crumbs
½ cup (125 ml) water
3 tablespoons (45 ml) chopped
  parsley
1 egg
1 small onion, grated

1½ teaspoon (7.5 ml) salt
Fresh ground pepper to taste
1 teaspoon (5 ml) Worcestershire
  sauce
1½ pounds (0.675 kg) ground
  beef
2 slices bacon

Mix bread, water, parsley, egg, onion and seasonings in a bowl until blended. Add ground beef and mix lightly together. Place meat mixture in 9 x 5 x 4-inch (22.5 x 12.5 x 10 cm) loaf pan or shape into a loaf on a shallow baking pan. Top with bacon slices. Bake at 350°F (175°C) — for 1½ hours. Serve hot or cold. Makes about 8 servings.

To make gravy: Remove meat loaf from pan. Pour drippings into a 2 cup (500 ml) measure. Spoon off most of the fat and add water to make 2 cups (500 ml) liquid. Mix 3 tablespoons (45 ml) flour with a little water to make a paste and stir into liquid. Cook and stir until gravy boils and is thickened. Taste for seasoning.

Beef-Pork Loaf: Substitute ½ pound (0.225 kg) ground pork for ½ pound (0.225 kg) beef. Omit bacon. Spread top of loaf with 3 tablespoons (45 ml) catsup or chili sauce.

Beef Sausage Loaf: Substitute ½ pound (0.225 kg) bulk country sausage for ½ pound (0.225 kg) ground beef. Omit bacon.

Herb Flavored Loaf: Substitute 1 cup (250 ml) herb flavored dressing mix for bread or bread crumbs.

Barbecue Loaf: Substitute ½ cup (125 ml) uncooked oatmeal for bread or bread crumbs. Spread top of loaf with ⅓ (80 ml) to ½ cup (125 ml) of your favorite barbecue sauce.

Tomato Loaf: Omit water and add 1 can (8 ounce—224 gm) tomato sauce and ½ teaspoon (2 ml) each dried basil and thyme.

Egg-A-Loaf: Hard cook 3 eggs and remove shells. Put half of the meat loaf mixture in loaf pan — lay eggs lengthwise, end to end down center of loaf, mold remaining meat loaf mixture around them and bake. When meat loaf is cut each slice will have egg in the center. This version can be done with any of the variations.

Classic Meat Loaf: Use proportion of ¾ pound (0.3375 kg) ground beef, ½ pound (0.225 kg) ground fresh pork, ½ pound (0.225 kg) ground veal. Use seasoning mixture as in basic meat loaf or herb loaf.

SUNDAY MEAT LOAF

Bake potatoes and a casserole of buttered asparagus while the meat loaf is baking.

1½ cups (375 ml) soft bread crumbs
½ teaspoon (2 ml) ground allspice
2 teaspoons (10 ml) salt
¼ teaspoon (1 ml) fresh ground
  pepper
2 tablespoons (30 ml) finely chopped
  onion

3 tablespoons (45 ml) finely chopped
  parsley
3 egg yolks
6 tablespoons (90 ml) dairy sour
  cream
4 tablespoons (60 ml) water
2 pounds (0.9 kg) ground beef

Combine bread crumbs with seasonings, egg yolk, sour cream and water in a large bowl. Blend well. Add beef and mix together lightly. Pack into a 9 x 5 x 4-inch (22.5 x 12.5 x 10 cm) loaf pan. Bake at 350°F (175°C) for 1½ hours. Makes 12 servings.

SAUSAGE LOAF

Put a casserole of scalloped potatoes in with the sausage loaf and also serve an apple salad.

1 cup (250 ml) coarsely crushed
    soda crackers
½ cup (125 ml) finely diced celery
¼ cup (50 ml) finely diced onion
½ cup (125 ml) catsup
½ teaspoon (2 ml) salt

¼ cup (50 ml) water
1 egg
1½ pounds (0.675 kg) bulk
    pork sausage
¾ pound (0.3375 kg) ground beef

In a large bowl mix crackers with celery, onion, catsup, salt, water and egg until well blended. Let stand about 5 minutes. Blend in sausage and beef. Pack into a 9 x 5 x 4-inch (22 x 12.5 x 10 cm) loaf pan and bake at 350°F (175°C) for 1½ hours. Makes 6 servings with leftovers.

GROUND BEEF PATTIES

One only has to witness the millions of hamburger palaces to know how popular hamburgers are. Plain — with cheese — with onion — with chili sauce. We will call them ground beef patties and give you a few variations. For the meat on the dinner menu, plan 2 or 3 patties to the pound (0.45 kg), for sandwiches, 4 or even 6, if other things are added. Shape the ground beef into patties with a light touch to keep the texture light. I like to heat the skillet on high — put in the patties and immediately turn the heat to moderate and finish on that temperature. For patties made 2 to the pound (0.45 kg) cook 5 minutes on each side for medium, shorter for rare, longer for well done. If the beef patties are made 3 to 6 to the pound (0.45 kg) they will be thinner and require less cooking. Salt and pepper before or after cooking.

Ground beef patties can also be broiled. Place patties on the broiler rack about 3-inches (7.5 cm) from the source of heat and cook 10 minutes, turning once, for medium.

A word about ground beef and hamburgers. The federal government (USDA) makes the following distinction between hamburger and ground beef: "Hamburger is ground beef to which seasonings and pieces of beef fat may be added while the meat is being ground. No added water, extenders or binders are permitted." "Ground beef" is ground beef — no extras, no binders or water — not even any fat. "Seasonings may be added as long as they are identified on the label."

Lightly spiced

For each pound (0.45 kg) of beef, add 1 teaspoon (5 ml) Worcestershire sauce, 1 teaspoon (5 ml) salt, 1 tablespoon (15 ml) grated or very finely chopped onion and fresh ground pepper to taste.

Mix the seasonings lightly into the ground beef and shape into patties.

Cheese

Prepare as for lightly spiced and add ½ cup (125 ml) grated American cheese.

Chili beef

Prepare as for lightly spiced and add 1 teaspoon (5 ml) chili powder, ¼ cup (50 ml) finely chopped green pepper.

Dennis Beef

For each pound (0.45 kg) ground beef mix in ½ cup (125 ml) soft bread crumbs, 1 teaspoon (5 ml) salt, ½ teaspoon (2 ml) poultry seasoning, 3 tablespoons (45 ml) water. Shape into 4 patties and cook 10 minutes, turning to brown both sides. Remove patties from pan, add ½ cup (125 ml) water. Cook and scrape brown from skillet. Serve with patties.

Waco beef

For each pound (0.45 kg) ground beef, add 1 clove mashed, garlic, 1 egg, 1 tablespoon (15 ml) prepared mustard, 2 teaspoons (10 ml) thick steak sauce, 1 teaspoon (5 ml) salt, fresh ground pepper to taste.

YUMMY BURGER SANDWICHES

French fries and chocolate malt will suit these sandwiches.

1 pound (0.45 kg) ground beef	¼ teaspoon (1 ml) garlic salt
1 medium onion, diced	¼ of a chili brick *or*
1 teaspoon (5 ml) salt	2 tablespoons (30 ml) tomato paste
Fresh ground pepper to taste	6 toasted hamburger buns

Combine beef, onion and seasonings in a skillet. Cover and cook over medium heat for about 20 minutes or until beef is lightly browned. Add cut up chili brick or tomato paste and simmer 5 to 10 minutes. Serve in toasted bun. Makes 6 servings.

CALIFORNIA BURGERS

French fries and fresh vegetable relishes would go well with these burgers.

2 pounds (0.9 kg) ground beef
1 teaspoon (5 ml) salt
½ teaspoon (2 ml) ground nutmeg
   or crushed cumin seed

½ cup (125 ml) finely chopped
   onion
¼ cup (50 ml) ice water
1 tablespoon (15 ml) butter
   or margarine

Combine all ingredients, mixing lightly. Form into oblong patties. Heat butter in skillet and cook patties about 5 minutes on each side for medium. Serve with Cold Sauce. Makes 6 servings.

Cold Sauce

2 cups (500 ml) peeled, chopped
   tomatoes
½ cup (125 ml) finely chopped onion
½ cup (125 ml) finely chopped canned
   peppers or fresh green peppers
1 teaspoon (5 ml) dried oregano

2 tablespoons (30 ml) wine vinegar
2 tablespoons (30 ml) olive oil
1 teaspoon (5 ml) salt
Fresh ground pepper to taste
6 drops Tabasco sauce

Combine all ingredients and chill well. Serve cold with meat. Makes 2 cups (500 ml) and will keep for several days in refrigerator.

INDOOR BARBECUE BEEF

The smoked salt gives an outdoor cooking flavor indoors. Serve on buns with shoestring potatoes.

1 pound (0.45 kg) ground beef
¼ cup (50 ml) finely chopped onion
1 teaspoon (5 ml) smoked salt
1 garlic clove, crushed
1 tablespoon (15 ml) brown sugar

1 tablespoon (15 ml) prepared mustard
¼ cup (50 ml) dry red wine
1 egg
1 tablespoon (15 ml) butter
   or margarine

Mix all ingredients except butter together lightly. Form into 4 patties. Heat butter in skillet and cook patties about 4 minutes on each side for medium. Makes 4 servings.

SPAGHETTI MEAT SAUCE

Many people will disagree with a spaghetti sauce which uses tomato sauce instead of tomato paste, but if you try this recipe you'll find it very good. Italian bread and mixed greens are my choice to serve with it.

1 tablespoon (15 ml) oil
1 clove garlic, minced
1 large onion, chopped
1 pound (0.45 kg) ground beef
1 teaspoon (5 ml) salt
Fresh ground pepper to taste
1 can (8 ounce – 227 gm) tomato sauce
1 tomato can water

½ teaspoon (2 ml) oregano
½ teaspoon (2 ml) basil
½ teaspoon (2 ml) thyme
1 clove, crushed in mortar
Dash Tabasco
1 teaspoon (5 ml) Worcestershire
   sauce
½ bay leaf
½ pound (0.225 kg) thin spaghetti,
   cooked as directed

Heat oil in skillet and cook garlic and onion until tender, but not browned. Add beef, break into small pieces, and continue cooking until lightly browned. Add remaining ingredients except spaghetti. Cover and simmer slowly for 1½–2 hours, adding additional water as needed. Serve with cooked thin spaghetti. Makes 2–3 servings.

MACARONI — MEAT SAUCE

Cold asparagus with mayonnaise and Italian bread will make this meal popular.

2 tablespoons (30 ml) oil
½ pound (0.225 kg) ground beef
½ pound (0.225 kg) ground
   fresh pork
1 medium onion, chopped
1 can (1 pound – 448 gm) tomatoes
1 can (8 ounce – 227 gm) tomato sauce
1 teaspoon (5 ml) salt

Fresh ground pepper to taste
½ teaspoon (2 ml) garlic salt
½ teaspoon (2 ml) celery salt
1 tablespoon (15 ml) Worcestershire
   sauce
1 package (8-ounce – 224 gm)
   macaroni
1 cup (250 ml) grated American Cheese

Heat oil and saute meats and onion for 10 minutes. Add tomatoes, tomato sauce and seasonings and simmer, covered, about 2 hours.

Cook macaroni as directed. Drain well. Spoon into a buttered 2 quart (1.9 L) flat casserole. Spoon sauce over macaroni and sprinkle with cheese. Bake at 400°F (204° C) for 15 minutes. Makes 4 to 6 servings.

BEEF AND CABBAGE CASSEROLE

Stuffed cabbage leaves are a Scandinavian treat, and a treat is this casserole which is a variation of the Scandinavian dish.

2 tablespoons (30 ml) butter or
   margarine
1 onion, chopped
½ pound (0.225 kg) ground beef
½ pound (0.225 kg) ground fresh pork
¼ teaspoon (1.25 ml) clove

1 teaspoon (5 ml) salt
Fresh ground pepper to taste
6 cups (1500 ml) coarsely chopped
   cabbage
1 can (10½ ounce – 294 gm)
   bouillon

Heat butter in skillet and saute onion until tender but not browned. Add beef and pork and saute until pink color is gone. If too much fat has accumulated, pour it off meat. (Leave about ¼ cup (50 ml)). Add seasonings, stirring to mix with meat. In a buttered 2½ quart (2.375 L) casserole put in ⅓ cabbage, then ½ meat and repeat, ending with a layer of cabbage. Pour bouillon over all. Cover and bake at 350°F (175°C) about 30 minutes or until cabbage is tender. Makes 4 to 6 servings.

BURGUNDY MEAT BALLS

Serve noodles and cucumber salad with meat balls.

1 pound (0.45 kg) ground beef
¼ pound (0.1125 kg) ground ham
½ cup (125 ml) Italian style
   bread crumbs
1 clove garlic, diced
2 tablespoons (30 ml) chopped parsley
½ teaspoon (2 ml) salt
Fresh ground pepper to taste
1 egg

¼ cup (50 ml) about, flour
2 tablespoons (30 ml) butter
   or margarine
1 large onion, diced
1 large tomato, peeled and diced
¼ teaspoon (1 ml) marjoram
¾ cup (180 ml) Burgundy wine
½ cup (125 ml) water

Mix together beef, ham, bread crumbs, garlic, parsley, salt, pepper and egg. Shape into 12–15 small balls. Roll in flour and brown in butter in large skillet. Remove from skillet as browned. Add onion and cook until tender. Add remaining ingredients to skillet, bring to a boil — add meat balls and simmer, covered, about 45 minutes. Add additional water if needed. Makes 4 to 6 servings.

SCOUT NIGHT CASSEROLE

This is really a meal in a dish. Serve bread and a fruit dessert.

1 pound (0.45 kg) ground beef
1 cup (250 ml) sliced celery
½ cup (125 ml) chopped onion
1 cup (250 ml) chopped green pepper
1 clove garlic, finely chopped
1½ cups (375 ml) water
¾ cup (180 ml) tomato paste
   (6-ounce (168 gm) can

¾ teaspoon (3.75 ml) salt
1 teaspoon (5 ml) chili powder
   (or more to taste)
2 cans (1 pound − 448 gm) each
   pork and beans
1 can (4 ounce − 112 gm) refrigerated
   baking powder biscuits

Combine beef with celery, onion, green pepper and garlic in large skillet and saute until vegetables are tender and meat lightly browned. (If there is excess fat pour it off.) Add water, tomato paste and seasonings and bring to a boil. Stir in beans and continue heating until beans are hot. Spoon into a 2½ quart (2.375 L) casserole. Top with biscuits. Bake at 375°F (190°C) 20 to 25 minutes or until biscuits are lightly browned. Makes 6 servings.

CREOLE BEEF AND RICE SKILLET

Pears with cottage cheese on shredded lettuce go well with this one-dish meal.

3 slices bacon, diced
1 medium onion, chopped
½ cup (125 ml) chopped green pepper
½ cup (125 ml) chopped celery
1 pound (0.45 kg) ground beef
1 teaspoon (5 ml) salt

1 can (1 pound − 448 gm) tomatoes
1 teaspoon (5 ml) basil
1 teaspoon (5 ml) oregano
⅛ teaspoon (0.5 ml) Tabasco
   sauce
½ cup (125 ml) long cooking rice

Pan fry bacon until crisp. Add onion, green pepper and celery and cook until tender, but not browned. Add ground beef, cook until red color is gone. Add remaining ingredients, stirring to mix. Cook covered about 30 minutes over low heat. Add water if needed. Makes 4 to 6 servings.

GROUND BEEF GOURMET

Serve with a green salad and bright julienne carrots. This makes a lovely quick dinner.

2 tablespoons (30 ml) butter
  or margarine
1 clove garlic, minced
1 onion, diced
1 cup (250 ml) fresh mushrooms,
  sliced
1 pound (0.45 kg) ground beef

1 teaspoon (5 ml) salt
Fresh ground pepper to taste
1 teaspoon (5 ml) dried rosemary
1 cup (250 ml) beef bouillon
⅔ cup (150 ml) dairy sour cream
1 pound (0.45 kg) medium noodles,
  cooked as directed

Heat butter in a skillet and saute garlic and onion until onion is tender. Add mushrooms and cook 5 minutes. Add beef and seasonings and continue cooking until meat is lightly browned. Stir in beef bouillon and sour cream and just heat, do not boil. Serve over hot cooked noodles. Makes 4 servings.

QUICK CASSEROLE DOROTHY

Add a fruit salad to this quickly prepared meal and take the compliments.

1 pound (0.45 kg) ground
  fresh pork
1 cup (250 ml) diced celery
1 cup (250 ml) diced green pepper

1 can (1 pound 4 ounce - 560 gm)
  spaghetti with tomato sauce
½ cup (125 ml) buttered
  bread crumbs
¼ cup (50 ml) grated American
  cheese

Saute ground pork in a skillet until lightly browned. With a slotted spoon remove pork to a bowl. Add celery and green pepper to skillet and cook until tender. Add with spaghetti to pork and mix lightly. Spoon into a buttered 2 quart (1.9 L) casserole. Top with buttered crumbs and sprinkle with grated cheese. Bake at 350°F (175°C) about 25 minutes. Makes 4 servings.

PORK-U-PINES

Serve spaghetti and zucchini and cole slaw with these tasty meat balls.

1 pound (0.45 kg) ground fresh pork
½ pound (0.225 kg) ground veal
¾ cup (180 ml) dry bread crumbs
1 egg
1 teaspoon (5 ml) salt

½ teaspoon (2 ml) paprika
¼ cup (50 ml) water
2 tablespoons (30 ml) soy sauce
¼ cup (50 ml) raw rice
2 cups (500 ml) spaghetti sauce
   without meat

Mix meats lightly with all ingredients except spaghetti sauce. Shape into small meat balls. Heat spaghetti sauce in a skillet. Drop in meat balls. Simmer about 45 minutes. Makes 6 servings.

LITTLE LAMB PATTIES WITH HERBED SAUCE

Serve rice or bulgar and green beans.

3 medium slices white bread, cubed
¼ cup (50 ml) water
1 egg
1 teaspoon (5 ml) salt
Fresh ground pepper to taste
½ teaspoon (2 ml) dried thyme
2 tablespoons (30 ml) grated onion
1 pound (0.45 kg) ground lamb

3 tablespoons (45 ml) butter
   or margarine
2 tablespoons (30 ml) flour
1½ cups (375 ml) bouillon
¼ teaspoon (1 ml) dried rosemary
3 tablespoons (45 ml) chopped parsley
½ teaspoon (2 ml) dried savory
3 tablespoons (45 ml) dry sherry

Combine bread with water, egg, salt, pepper, thyme and onion. Blend well. Add lamb and mix lightly. Shape lamb into 12 small patties. Heat butter in skillet and brown lamb patties on both sides, removing to plate as browned. When all are browned add flour to skillet. Stir in bouillon and cook and scrape brown crust from bottom of pan. Add remaining ingredients and bring to a boil. Return lamb patties to sauce in skillet and cook over low heat 30 minutes. Serve with hot cooked rice or bulgar. Makes 4 servings.

Hot buttered rice and green beans amandine will help to make this a feast. Serve a relish tray of cherry tomatoes, celery and cucumber sticks.

2 medium slices bread, cubed
¼ cup (50 ml) milk
1 egg
½ teaspoon (2 ml) dry mustard
½ teaspoon (2 ml) ginger
½ teaspoon (2 ml) salt
2 tablespoons (30 ml) soy sauce
1 pound (0.45 kg) ground lamb

3 to 4 tablespoons (45–60 ml) flour
2 tablespoons (30 ml) oil
1 cup (250 ml) pineapple juice
2 tablespoons (30 ml) brown sugar
½ cup (125 ml) diced green pepper
½ cup (125 ml) pineapple chunks
¼ cup (50 ml) vinegar

Combine bread with milk, egg, mustard, ginger, salt and soy sauce and blend well. Mix lamb in lightly and shape into 12 to 15 small balls. Roll in flour and brown in oil. Add remaining ingredients. Cook, stirring occasionally, for 30–35 minutes. Serve with sauce. Makes 4 to 6 servings.

Use human rather than automatic dishwasher.

SPICE UP A MENU WITH VARIETY MEATS

Liver, Tongue, Kidney, Brains, Tripe and Sweetbreads are among the items in the meat market that are commonly known as specialty or variety meats. They are all highly nutritious and, in many cases, relatively inexpensive per serving.

For the young homemaker I would suggest introducing these foods to your children as soon as the pediatrician will let you so that they do not grow up getting negative impressions from others who do not like them.

Liver comes in veal, calf, lamb, beef and pork. Veal liver is the most expensive and mild flavored, but calves (sometimes it will be called "baby beef") is a fine tasting liver. Lamb livers are smaller, but equal to veal and calf in flavor. Those three can be pan fried, pan broiled or broiled. If beef liver comes from a young enough beef it might be treated as the first three, but you'd better plan on braising. Pork liver is stronger in flavor and should always be braised.

Tongues come fresh, pickled, smoked, cooked and uncooked, canned and jarred. Beef tongues are more likely to come in the first categories, lamb tongue in jars. Tongue is best cooked by simmering in water, then when tender, cool, remove the skin and roots. It is good either hot or cold.

Kidneys are considered a delicacy and the most delicate are veal and lamb. Beef kidney is less tender than veal and lamb. Always remove the membrane and cut out the hard parts of the kidney. Lamb kidneys can be left whole.

Brains are a delicately flavored part of the animal. They can be parboiled before preparing the recipe or not. However if they are not to be used at once they should always be parboiled for refrigerator storage regardless of preparation.

Method. Wash carefully and remove the membrane before or after parboiling. Simmer 15 to 20 minutes.

Tripe, the lining of the calves stomach, can be purchased fresh, pickled or canned. It is delicately flavored but tough and requires long slow cooking in water.

Sweetbreads are the two lobes of the thymus gland and are highly prized by conoisseurs of haut cuisine. They come from veal and young beef and can be broiled, fried, braised or cooked in liquid.

1 fresh beef tongue, 2 to 5
  pounds (0.9 – 2.25 kg)
1 to 2 teaspoons (5 to 10 ml) salt
1 bay leaf
3 or 4 whole cloves

1 large onion, sliced
1 stalk celery
1 carrot, peeled
6 peppercorns

Wash tongue and put in a large Dutch oven. Cover with cold water and add seasonings. Bring to a boil, cover, and simmer until tender, about 3 to 4 hours. Remove from liquid, cool in cold water just enough to handle and remove skin at once. Slit skin on underside, thick end to tip. Pull skin off all in one piece. Trim muscle at large end.

Tongue may be served hot or cold. It may also have vegetables cooked with it as in a New England dinner. About 30 minutes before the tongue is done add peeled potatoes, small white onions, peeled carrots and cabbage sufficient for the number of people you are serving. Serve horseradish and mustard with tongue.

* If tongue is pickled or cured omit salt.

Sour cream horseradish sauce: Mix ½ cup (125 ml) dairy sour cream with 4 tablespoons (60 ml) horseradish, 1 teaspoon (5 ml) lemon juice and salt to taste.

Mustard cream sauce: Whip ½ cup (125 ml) heavy cream and fold in 2 tablespoons (30 ml) prepared mustard and 1 tablespoon (15 ml) horseradish.

Currant Orange sauce: Break up ½ cup (125 ml) currant jelly and add 2 tablespoons (30 ml) frozen orange juice, ¾ teaspoon (3 ml) dry mustard, 1 tablespoon vinegar. Blend well.

Liver and deep yellow and green vegetables provide the best source of Vitamin A.

MOCK TERRAPIN

This delicious way to serve liver should become a favorite. Mashed potatoes and peas and celery go well with it. Add a cranberry relish.

1 pound (0.45 kg) beef liver
   cut in ½-inch (1.25 cm) slices
Instant meat tenderizer
2 tablespoons (30 ml) bacon fat
   or butter
1 tablespoon (15 ml) flour

1 cup (250 ml) water
¼ teaspoon (1 ml) Tabasco Sauce
1 tablespoon (15 ml) prepared mustard
Salt and fresh ground pepper
   to taste
2 hard cooked eggs, peeled and diced

Sprinkle liver with meat tenderizer as directed on label. Heat bacon fat in skillet and quickly sear liver on both sides until lightly browned. Remove from skillet and cool enough to dice liver in about ¼-inch (0.625 cm) cubes. Set aside. Add flour to fat in skillet and stir to loosen crust. Add water, Tabasco and mustard and cook and stir over low heat until thickened. Season to taste with salt and pepper. Add liver and eggs and cook about 2 minutes. Makes 4 servings.

CALVES LIVER AND BACON

One of the tastiest meals is properly cooked calves liver. I think it is best if sliced as thinly as possible. If it is not possible to buy it other than in already thick slices, partially freeze the slices and with a sharp knife cut them crosswise into thin slices. Some people prefer to dip the liver into flour seasoned with salt and pepper — others cook it bare. If you haven't already made up your mind, try both methods and decide yourself. Boiled potatoes with melted butter and paprika or chopped parsley and a watercress salad make good accompaniments.

8 slices bacon
1 pound (0.45 kg) sliced calves
   liver

3 to 4 tablespoons (45 to 60 ml) flour
Salt and fresh ground pepper to
   taste

Cook bacon in a large skillet, and remove from skillet as it is lightly browned and keep hot. Dip liver slices in flour seasoned with salt and pepper and fry quickly in bacon fat, turning to brown both sides (about 6 minutes altogether). Serve liver with bacon. Makes 4 servings.

Veal, calves and some beef liver may also be broiled. Dip liver to be broiled in melted butter, margarine or bacon fat. Broil about 3 minutes on each side.

TRIPE WITH CHICK PEAS

This is a Portuguese recipe even tripe haters will like. Serve hot cooked rice and an orange salad with it.

1 pound (0.45 kg) dried chick peas
1 pound (0.45 kg) fresh tripe
   (not pickled)
2 tablespoons (30 ml) olive oil
2 onions, chopped
2 carrots, peeled and diced

2 tomatoes, peeled and diced
1 bay leaf
½ pound (0.225 kg) bacon or
   smoked sausage
1½ teaspoons (7 ml) salt
Fresh ground pepper to taste

Pick over and wash chick peas. Soak over night in water to cover. The next day, combine chick peas and water in which they were soaked and tripe in a large saucepan. If necessary add additional water to cover. Bring to a boil and simmer about 2 hours or until the tripe and peas are tender. Remove the tripe from the saucepan and cut it into inch (2.5 cm) squares. Heat olive oil in a skillet. Add onions, carrots and tomatoes and cook, stirring, until onions are lightly browned. Add bay leaf. Add bacon or sausage, cut into inch (2.5 cm) pieces and continue cooking until bacon or sausage is completely cooked. Add salt and pepper.

With a slotted spoon, remove chick peas from liquid and add with tripe to vegetable mixture. Add some of the liquid in which tripe and peas were cooked. Simmer 15 minutes. Remove bay leaf and serve. Makes 4 to 6 servings.

SAUTEED SWEETBREADS WITH MUSHROOMS

Serve with asparagus and Hollandaise sauce.

3 pairs sweetbreads
1 tablespoon (15 ml) lemon juice
Salt
4 tablespoons (60 ml) butter
   or margarine
2 cups (500 ml) thinly sliced
   mushrooms

1 egg
⅓ cup (75 ml) dried bread
   crumbs
4 tablespoons (60 ml) butter
   or margarine, melted
1 lemon

Soak sweetbreads in cold water for 30 minutes. Discard water.

Remove all membrane. Add lemon juice and 1 teaspoon (5 ml) salt per quart (1000 ml) of water needed to cover sweetbreads and simmer for 15 minutes. Drain.

Heat butter in a skillet and gently cook mushrooms until lightly browned. Remove from skillet and keep hot. Cut sweetbreads into 6 pieces and dip in egg and crumbs. Pan fry in butter in skillet until browned, turning to brown both sides. Serve with sauteed mushrooms, melted butter and slices of fresh lemon. Makes 6 servings.

74

BRAINS AND SCRAMBLED EGGS

This is one of the most popular ways in which brains are served. It can be a luncheon, supper or breakfast dish and what is served with it depends on the meal. For breakfast — half canteloupe or citrus fruit in season and toasted English muffins and strawberry jam.

1 brain (about ½ pound-0.225 kg)
1 tablespoon (15 ml) lemon juice
1 teaspoon (5 ml) salt
4 eggs
4 tablespoons (60 ml) water

½ teaspoon (2 ml) salt
Fresh ground pepper to taste
4 tablespoons (60 ml) butter
   or margarine
4 tablespoons (60 ml) chopped
   fresh parsley

Remove membrane from brains and wash. Cover with water, to which has been added lemon juice and 1 teaspoon (5 ml) salt. Bring to a boil and simmer 20 minutes. Drain and cut into small pieces.

Gently mix eggs with water, ½ teaspoon (2 ml) salt and pepper. Heat butter in skillet and add brains and cook, stirring until lightly browned. Add eggs and continue cooking, stirring carefully from bottom until eggs are just set. Spoon onto platter and sprinkle parsley over eggs. Makes 4 servings.

KIDNEYS IN RED WINE

This simple recipe is good made with beef, veal or lamb kidneys. I make it with whichever I can find in the meat market though it was originally developed for veal. Serve the kidneys over rice and add green beans amandine and tossed salad.

2 beef or 4 veal or lamb kidneys
3 tablespoons (45 ml) flour
½ teaspoon (2 ml) salt
Fresh ground pepper to taste

3 tablespoons (45 ml) butter
   or margarine
1 clove garlic, diced
1½ cups (375 ml) dry red wine
   (burgundy, Chianti)
Hot steamed rice

Wash kidneys and cut out all the fat and hard parts. Slice into thin slices. Mix flour with salt and pepper and sprinkle over kidneys. Heat butter with garlic for a few minutes. Add kidneys and saute quickly, about 3 minutes, stirring. Add red wine and bring to a boil and simmer 5 minutes. Serve over rice. Makes 4 to 6 servings.

TRY TASTE-TEMPTING SAUSAGES

Would you even guess that under the classification of Sausage there are more than 200 different kinds? Everything from Bologna to Souse! And what a wonderful world of flavor it is. Many of the varieties are European in origin — some from our ingenious development. All are spiced with a verve and flair that would make Marco Polo proud. Produced with the most modern care they will enhance meals summer and winter. You will be met with such names as Cervelat, Mortadella, Peppered loaf, Olive loaf, Honey loaf, Pickle and Pimiento loaf to name a few. These are in addition to the well known terms — bologna, braunschweiger, frankfurters, salami, Polish sausage (Kielbasa).

We will be able to cover only a small portion of the varieties. It is suggested that when you find a variety with which you are not familiar, buy the smallest quantity possible the first time. This gives you the opportunity to taste-test and it may turn out to be a favorite addition to your cold cut list after that sampling.

Sausage comes in two broad categories.

(1) Those which are fresh and or smoked and need cooking or heating before eaten.

(2) Ready-to-serve sausages and luncheon meats which are sliced and served cold without further cooking.

Sausages are made from minced or ground meats, usually seasoned with salt and spices and stuffed into a casing. They may be fresh or smoked, dry or semi-dry, uncooked, partially cooked, or fully cooked. Sausages make up about 15% of all the red meat consumed in this country.

Breakfast Sausage comes in links and as bulk sausage. What we call "bulk" sausage is generally in a casing about 6 inches (15 cm) long. It can be sliced crosswise into patties or removed from the casing to be used in other forms. Breakfast sausage must be cooked before eating.

Breakfast sausage, which we meet first in the day, can be cooked several different ways. You might like to try each and choose your favorite.

1. Place links or patties in a cold skillet. Add 2 to 4 teaspoons (10 – 20 ml) water, cover tightly and cook slowly 5 to 8 minutes. Remove cover, pour off water and fat and continue cooking slowly until well done and nicely browned, turning occasionally.
2. Place sausages in a single layer in a shallow baking pan. Bake at 400°F (200°C) 20 – 30 minutes or until well done. Pour off drippings as they accumulate.
3. Cover links or patties with cold water. Bring to a boil and simmer 10 minutes. Drain and brown lightly on medium heat.

Quick Tricks with Sausage

Orange Sauce: Pan fry sausage with 2−4 teaspoons (10−20 ml) water. When sausage is done, pour off all but 2 tablespoons (30 ml) fat. Add ¼ cup (50 ml) orange marmalade, a dash of prepared mustard and 2 tablespoons (30 ml) orange juice. Heat, stirring, and serve with sausage.

Cranberry Sauce: Pan fry sausage with 2−4 teaspoons (10−20 ml) water. When sausage is done, pour off all but 2 tablespoons (30 ml) fat. Add ½ cup (125 ml) whole cranberry sauce and a dash each of cinnamon and nutmeg. Heat, stirring, and serve with sausage.

Sausage 'n' Egg Scramble

Cut ½ pound (0.225 kg) link sausage into ½-inch pieces or crumble bulk sausage. Pan fry with 2−4 teaspoons (10−20 ml) water. Add ½ cup (125 ml) diced green pepper and 1 small onion chopped and cook until tender. Pour off all but about 2 tablespoons (30 ml) of fat and add 5 or 6 eggs mixed with 4 tablespoons (60 ml) water, ¼ teaspoon (1 ml) salt and fresh ground pepper to taste. Cook and stir over medium heat until eggs are set. Serve with toasted English muffins. Makes 4 servings.

Sausage — Corn Pancakes

Cut ½ pound (0.225 kg) link sausage into ½-inch (1.25 cm) pieces or crumble bulk sausage and pan fry until lightly browned. Prepare corn pancakes as directed on an 8½ ounce (238 gm) package of corn muffin mix. Stir cooked sausage into batter and bake on griddle as directed on package. Serve with maple sirup. Makes 10−12 pancakes.

But breakfast sausage doesn't need to stop at the breakfast table. There are many interesting ways it can fit into other meals.

Match pan size to the size of the heating unit and select pans with tight-fitting lids.

SAUSAGE VEGETABLE PIE

Serve a cranberry relish/salad with this one dish meal.

1½ pounds (0.675 kg) bulk sausage
2 cups (500 ml) diced potatoes
1 cup (250 ml) diced turnips
1 cup (250 ml) cooked peas
1 cup (250 ml) diced carrots

1 onion, cut in thin slices
2 tablespoons (30 ml) flour
1 teaspoon (5 ml) salt
2 cups (500 ml) water
1 can refrigerated biscuits

Make sausage into small patties and brown lightly in a skillet. Lightly mix potatoes with turnips, peas and carrots and spoon into a buttered 2-quart (1.9 L) casserole. Arrange onion slices on top and then sausage patties.

Add flour to fat in skillet and cook and stir to remove any crust from the pan. Add salt and water and heat to boiling. Pour over sausage and vegetables in casserole. Cover (with aluminum foil, if casserole does not have a lid). Bake at 350°F (175°C) for about 45 minutes or until vegetables are tender. Top with biscuits and continue baking about 20 minutes longer or until biscuits are brown. Makes 6 servings.

SAUSAGE SURPRISE

Try this combination for lunch when the occasion calls for a little more than a sandwich. Serve cole slaw with it.

1 pound (0.45 kg) link sausage
4 medium sweet potatoes or yams
2 tablespoons (30 ml) butter or
    margarine
½ teaspoon (2 ml) salt

2 tablespoons (30 ml) brown sugar
Milk
4 slices pineapple
½ cup (125 ml) buttered bread
    crumbs

Pan fry sausages until lightly browned. Cook sweet potatoes in boiling salted water. Peel and mash with butter, salt, brown sugar and enough milk to make fluffy. Place pineapple slices in a well buttered flat baking dish. Place 2 or 3 sausages on each pineapple slice and cover with mashed sweet potato. Sprinkle with crumbs. Bake at 375°F (190°C) for 15–20 minutes. Bake this dish in individual ramekins if you have them. Makes 4 servings.

SAUSAGE SKILLET

Serve peas and a tossed salad with the Sausage Skillet.

1 pound (0.45 kg) link or bulk
   sausage
1½ cups (375 ml) pre-cooked rice
1 medium onion, chopped
2 stalks celery, chopped

¾ cup (180 ml) bouillon
¾ cup (180 ml) dry white wine
Salt and fresh ground pepper
   to taste

Cut link sausage into 1-inch pieces or, if using bulk sausage, crumble it. Pan fry in a large skillet until lightly browned. Remove sausage to a dish and pour off all but about 2 tablespoons (30 ml) fat. Add rice and vegetables and cook slowly, stirring until lightly browned. Add sausage meat, bouillon, wine and salt and pepper to taste. Bring to a boil and simmer 15 – 20 minutes. Makes 4 servings.

QUICK SPAGHETTI SAUCE

Make an Italian salad with red onion slices and sliced beets to serve with this spaghetti — along with the usual crusty bread.

1 pound (0.45 kg) sweet or hot
   Italian sausage
1 large onion, chopped
1 can (8-ounce (224 gm) tomato
   sauce

1 tomato sauce can water
1 pound (0.45 kg) thin spaghetti,
   cooked
Grated Parmesan cheese, if desired

Cut sausage crosswise into ½-inch (1.25 cm) pieces. Fry in a skillet with onion until sausage is lightly browned and onions tender. Pour off fat. Add tomato sauce and water and simmer, covered, about 30 minutes. Serve with spaghetti and cheese. Makes 4 servings.

SAUSAGE AND CORN PUDDING

Buttered beets and a jellied perfection salad are suggested to go with this casserole.

1 pound (0.45 kg) bulk sausage
6 slices bread
1 can (12-ounce (336 gm) whole
   kernel corn, drained
1 tablespoon (15 ml) grated onion

1 teaspoon (5 ml) prepared
   mustard
3 eggs
1¼ cups (300 ml) milk
½ cup (125 ml) grated cheese

Crumble sausage and pan fry until lightly browned. Cut bread slices diagonally and arrange half of the slices in a well buttered 1½ quart (1.43 L) flat 9 x 9-inch (22.5 x 22.5 cm) casserole. Spoon half sausage and half corn on bread and repeat. Mix seasonings with eggs and milk. Pour carefully over bread and sausage in casserole. Sprinkle with cheese. Let stand at least 30 minutes in refrigerator and then bake at 325°F (160°C) 1 hour or until set. Makes 4 to 6 servings.

SAUSAGE WITH SAUERKRAUT

Buttered noodles and parslied carrots fill out the menu.

1½ pound (0.675 kg) smoked country
   style sausage
1 can (27 oz. − 765 gm) sauerkraut
1 tart apple, peeled and diced
1 small onion

5 cloves
1 teaspoon (5 ml) caraway seed
2 tablespoons (30 ml) brown
   sugar

Cut sausage into serving size pieces. Combine sauerkraut with apple, onion in which cloves have been stuck, caraway seed and brown sugar in a large saucepan. Place sausage pieces on top of sauerkraut. Bring to a boil, cover, and simmer for about 1 hour over low heat. Makes 4 servings.

Meat is high in protein in relation to calories and needed for growth and maintenance of the body.

SCALLOPED POLISH SAUSAGE AND POTATOES

5 medium potatoes
1 pound (0.45 kg) Polish sausage
1 large onion, sliced
2 tablespoons (30 ml) flour

1 teaspoon (5 ml) salt
2 cups (500 ml) milk
2 tablespoons (30 ml) butter or
  margarine

Peel and thinly slice potatoes. Remove skin from sausage, if any, and slice into thin slices. Arrange alternate layers of potato, onion and sausage in a buttered 2 quart (2.375 L) casserole. Sprinkle each layer with some of the flour and salt. Heat milk and pour over potatoes in casserole so that it comes up just below top slices. Dot with butter. Cover and bake at 350°F (175°C) about 30 minutes. Uncover and bake 30 minutes longer or until potatoes are tender and browned. Makes 4 to 6 servings.

BARLEY SCRAPPLE

This dish never gets set up like scrapple made with cornmeal, but if you like barley it is a marvelous dish for cold winter breakfasts. Start with fruit juice and your favorite beverage.

2 pounds (0.9 kg) lean pork or
  2 fresh pork hocks
1 bay leaf

4 peppercorns
1 teaspoon (5 ml) salt
1 pound (448 gm) pearl barley

The day before this dish is to be put together, combine pork, bay leaf, peppercorns and salt in a saucepan. Cover with water and bring to a boil. Simmer covered, until tender, about 1 hour. Cool. Remove meat from bone (if fresh pork hocks are used, discard skin) and grind or chop coarsely. Strain broth.

Wash barley and soak overnight in water. The next day, combine broth and meat with barley and water in which it was soaked in a large, heavy saucepan. Simmer, covered, until barley is tender, about 3 hours. Add water as needed but toward end of cooking time do not add too much as barley mixture should be thick. Stir often. If barley seems to be sticking, shut off heat and let stand 5 to 10 minutes until steamed loose from bottom. Then continue cooking.

To serve: Put cooked barley in refrigerator and chill well. Heat a generous amount of butter or margarine in skillet and add enough of the barley to serve the desired number of people. Pan fry until hot. The barley will keep under refrigeration for about 2 weeks and this amount makes enough for 10 – 12 servings.

Frankfurters

Frankfurters are perhaps the most widely sold sausage of them all. Famous for their popularity at the sports stadiums, they are equally a staple in most homes.

Read the labels and try the different varieties to choose the ones that will be your favorites.

Frankfurters are fully cooked but the flavor is improved by heating. They can be heated in several ways. Serve with mustard, catsup, pickle relish and/or chopped onion.

1. Cover with water, bring to a boil and simmer just below boiling point about 8 minutes.
2. Put a small amount of butter or margarine in a skillet and brown frankfurters on all sides over medium heat.
3. Split frankfurters lengthwise almost through. Brown cut sides in a small amount of butter or margarine, turn and brown other sides. Frankfurters heated this way fit into sandwich bread if you don't have buns.

Frankfurters can also be heated in other liquids beside water. Heated in beer they have a completely different flavor or heated in sauerkraut and its juice is a favorite with a lot of people. Knockwurst or Bratwurst is particularly popular this way.

B B Q sauce is also used for heating frankfurters.

Tuck the hot frankfurters in a toasted bun and you've a grand sandwich.

Some appealing food combinations with frankfurters:

Frankfurters and beans (baked beans is the one thought of first, but frankfurters are also good with dried or fresh lima beans, kidney beans, just plain boiled dried beans, or yellow eye beans).

Frankfurters, potato salad and sliced tomatoes
Frankfurters and big hominy
Frankfurters and lentils
Frankfurters and macaroni and cheese
Frankfurters and scalloped potatoes

STRETCH-A-FRANK FILLING

1 cup (250 ml) chopped or ground
  frankfurters
3 tablespoons (45 ml) pickle relish

1 tablespoon (15 ml) prepared
  mustard
¼ cup (50 ml) mayonnaise

Mix all ingredients. Chill well. Makes 1 cup (250 ml) or filling for 4 to 5 sandwiches.

SUPER FRANKS

Potato chips and a vanilla milk shake go with these fancy franks.

12 frankfurters
Barbecue sauce (thick)
8 ounces (224 gm) American
  cheese

4 good sized dill pickles
6 slices bacon
12 frankfurter rolls

Slit frankfurters lengthwise almost through. Spread cut side generously with barbecue sauce. Cut cheese and pickles into 12 strips the same length as franks. Put a strip of each in frank. Cut bacon crosswise in 12 pieces. Close franks around pickle and cheese as much as possible and wrap a slice of bacon around each frank, fastening each end with toothpick. Broil, turning, to cook bacon crisp and melt cheese. Remove toothpicks and serve in toasted buns. Makes 12.

MACARONI AND FRANKS

1 package (8 oz–224 gm) elbow
  macaroni
1 cup (250 ml) milk
2 eggs
1 cup (250 ml) grated American
  cheese

1 teaspoon (5 ml) salt
1 tablespoon (15 ml) chopped
  parsley
6 frankfurters
½ cup (125 ml) buttered crumbs

Cook macaroni as directed on package. Drain. Mix milk, eggs, cheese, salt and parsley. Cut frankfurters in ½-inch pieces, crosswise. Combine cooked macaroni, frankfurters and egg mixture. Spoon into a buttered 6 cup casserole. Sprinkle with buttered crumbs. Bake at 350°F (175°C) for 30 minutes or until egg mixture is set.

NOODLED FRANKS

Add green beans and a fruit salad for a complete menu.

1 pound (0.45 kg) frankfurters
2 tablespoons (30 ml) butter
   or margarine
1 cup (250 ml) thinly sliced onion

1 cup (250 ml) uncooked noodles
1 can (10¾ oz. − 301 gm) tomato
   soup
1 soup can water

Slice frankfurters crosswise into thin slices. In a large skillet, pan fry in butter with onions 5 minutes. Add remaining ingredients and stir and mix together. Bring to a boil, cover and simmer 30 minutes or until noodles are tender. Makes 4−6 servings.

FRANKFURTER KABOBS

Sometimes its fun to make frankfurter kabobs to broil in place of plain franks. Use our suggestions for kabob — but dream up some of your own. Potato salad and assorted vegetable relishes are good with kabobs.

6 frankfurters
2 to 3 dill or sweet pickles
12 cherry tomatoes
12 chunks cooked carrot
¼ cup (50 ml) oil

2 tablespoons (30 ml) vinegar
   or pickle juice
1 tablespoon (15 ml) prepared
   mustard
¼ teaspoon (1 ml) salt

Cut frankfurters crosswise into about 1½-inch (3.75 cm) chunks. Cut pickles into 1-inch (2.5 cm) chunks. String franks, pickle chunks, cherry tomatoes and cooked carrot chunks on 4 skewers. Mix oil with vinegar, mustard and salt. Brush kabobs with mixture before and during cooking. Broil about 2-inches (5 cm) from source of heat, about 10 minutes, turning to brown all sides. Makes 4 servings.

FRANKFURTERS IN BARBECUE SAUCE

You can heat frankfurters in your favorite commercial barbecue sauce or make your own. Here is a make-your-own when you have time. It's especially good and good with it is steamed rice and green beans.

1 medium onion, chopped
1 clove garlic, chopped
2 tablespoons (30 ml) butter or
   margarine
2 tablespoons (30 ml) vinegar
2 tablespoons (30 ml) brown sugar
4 tablespoons (50 ml) lemon juice

1 cup (250 ml) catsup
3 tablespoons (45 ml) Worcestershire sauce
2 teaspoons (10 ml) prepared
   mustard
½ cup (125 ml) water
½ cup (125 ml) chopped celery
1½ pounds (0.675 kg) frankfurters

Saute onion and garlic in butter. Add remaining ingredients except frankfurters. Cook and stir to blend and bring to a boil. Simmer, covered, about 30 minutes. Add frankfurters and simmer 30 minutes longer. Serve frankfurters with sauce. Makes 6 servings.

Adults need for protein remains about the same from age 21 on.

BACON FROM SUNUP TO SUNDOWN

Bacon is prepared from the breast and flank of the pork. The bones are removed and sold as spareribs. The remainder is trimmed, cured and smoked and sold as bacon. (It is also the area from which salt pork is made.)

Bacon is primarily sold pre-sliced and packaged. However, it can be purchased uncut and often bacon is store-sliced and packaged.

There is also Canadian-style bacon which is cured and smoked boneless loin of pork. It is very low in fat and can be sliced and pan fried or broiled.

Remember buying by cost per serving when bacon is concerned. Most packaged bacon is cut 18 slices to the pound. If 2 slices are a serving and bacon costs $1.89 a pound, this means each slice costs 10 cents. But if you watch for bacon bargains it can even be less in cost per slice. It is so versatile in use it adds flavor to many chicken and meat dishes.

Once a package of bacon is purchased, use it within a week or ten days for very best flavor. To cook to eat as "bacon", it can be either pan fried, oven cooked, or broiled.

1. *Pan fry:* Put bacon strips in a cold skillet and fry over medium heat, turning often, until crisp. Pour off fat as bacon cooks. But don't discard, save bacon fat for cooking.
2. *Broil:* Place bacon strips on broiler rack and broil 2−3 inches (5−7.5 cm) from heat, 3 to 4 minutes.
3. *Oven cooked:* Place bacon strips on rack in shallow baking pan and bake at 350°F (175°C) 20 to 25 minutes.

To cook Canadian bacon:

Pan fry or pan broil: Over moderate heat, ½-inch (1.25 cm) thick slices of Canadian-style bacon, turning to brown meat on both sides, about 6 minutes total cooking time. A small amount of fat may need to be added. However, if fat should accumulate during cooking, pour it off.

Broil: 3 to 5 inches (7.5−12.5 cm) from source of heat, broil ¼-inch (0.625 cm) thick slices 6−8 minutes total; ½-inch (1.25 cm) thick slices 8−10 minutes.

My mother always had a container on the back of the stove in which she poured the bacon fat. It was used for everything from frying eggs to seasoning cabbage. Today we can save our bacon fat in containers in the freezer, which we should do, since it is versatile and can be used any place where bacon flavor is compatible.

It can be used to season all vegetables and is particularly good with cabbage and its relatives.

Bacon fat is exceptionally good for frying fish.

Use it as the shortening in pancakes.

Use half lard and half bacon fat for frying chicken.

Using bacon to flavor

When cooking fresh green beans add a few slices of diced bacon.

Black-eye peas seasoned with cut up bacon while cooking are wonderful.

Cut up some bacon, fry until crisp and mix into your favorite cornbread batter before baking.

Use diced bacon instead of salt pork in fish chowder.

Sprinkle some crisply cooked, crumbled bacon over boiled cabbage.

Crisply cook several bacon slices, crumble. Pour off all but 2 to 3 tablespoons (30−45 ml) fat. Add a can of drained whole kernel corn and heat.

Brown cooked sweet potatoes or yams in bacon fat. Sprinkle with crisp crumbled bacon to serve.

BACON AND EGGS

1. Cook bacon as desired. When done keep hot. Add 2 to 3 (30 to 45 ml) tablespoons bacon fat to skillet, let warm a few minutes and drop in eggs. Fry to desired doneness over moderate heat. To cook white over yolks, either flip the egg with a pancake turner or put a lid on the skillet so the egg tops steam-cook.

2. If you prefer scrambled eggs, break the desired number in a bowl (1½ eggs per person) add 1 tablespoon (15 ml) water, a dash of salt and fresh ground pepper to taste for each egg. (You may use milk, but water makes for a more tender egg.) Mix together lightly — do not beat. Heat 2 to 3 tablespoons (30 to 45 ml) bacon fat in the skillet. Pour in egg mixture and cook, using a spoon to pull in cooked eggs from outer edge of skillet, until of desired consistency.

BACON AND EGG SANDWICHES

Makes a good lunch with carrot sticks and a glass of milk.

8 slices bacon
4 eggs

Salt and fresh ground pepper
to taste
8 slices buttered toast

Cook bacon in a large skillet until the desired crispness. Pour off all but 2 or 3 tablespoons (30−45 ml) bacon fat. Arrange slices of bacon in pairs of 2. Either break each egg into a custard cup and scramble white and yolk with a fork, then pour over bacon slices, or break egg onto bacon slices and break yolk with a fork. Season with salt and pepper. Fry until eggs begin to set, then with a spatula, turn and fry other side. Serve between 2 slices of buttered toast.

BACON "WESTERN"

Chopped ham is the usual Western, but this is a good variation. Serve with a cup of tomato soup.

8 slices bacon
2 tablespoons (30 ml) finely
  chopped onion
3 tablespoons (45 ml) finely
  chopped green pepper
5 eggs, slightly beaten

3 tablespoons (45 ml) water
¾ teaspoon (3 ml) salt
Fresh ground pepper to taste
8 slices buttered bread or toast

Dice bacon and fry in skillet until crisp. Pour off all but 2 to 3 tablespoons (30–45 ml) fat. Mix onion, green pepper, eggs, water, salt and pepper. Mix into skillet with bacon and cook over moderate heat until firm. Spoon onto toast and add other half to make a sandwich. Makes 4 sandwiches.

GRILLED PEANUT BUTTER AND BACON SANDWICH

Another winner. Serve with a glass of chocolate milk.

4 slices bacon
⅔ cup (150 ml) peanut butter
4 tablespoons (60 ml) mayonnaise

3 tablespoons (45 ml) pickle
  relish
8 slices bread

Cook bacon in skillet until desired doneness. Cut slices in half crosswise. Pour off all but 2 to 3 tablespoons (30–45 ml) fat.

Mix peanut butter with mayonnaise and pickle relish. Spread 4 slices of bread with mixture. Add 1 slice of bacon and top with another slice of bread. Heat bacon fat in skillet and grill sandwiches over medium heat, turning to brown both sides. Add additional bacon fat when sandwiches are turned, if necessary. Makes 4 sandwiches.

SPAGHETTI WITH BACON SAUCE

This is a wonderful quickie when needed. Italian bread and spinach salad would make the menu complete.

½ pound (225 gm) diced bacon
1 onion, thinly sliced
3 cups (750 ml) peeled and chopped
   tomatoes
1 tablespoon (15 ml) tomato paste

1 teaspoon (5 ml) dried marjoram
Salt and fresh ground pepper
   to taste
1 pound (0.45 kg) thin spaghetti,
   cooked as directed
Parmesan cheese

Cook bacon in skillet until crisp. Add onion and cook until transparent. Add tomatoes, tomato paste and marjoram. Cook 15 minutes. Add salt and fresh ground pepper to taste. Serve on hot cooked spaghetti with Parmesan cheese. Makes 4 servings.

BEANS 'N' BACON

A good supper dish when served with brown bread and cole slaw.

6 slices bacon
1 large onion, chopped
½ cup (125 ml) finely chopped
   green pepper

½ cup (125 ml) tomato sauce
2 tablespoons (30 ml) molasses
2 cans (1 pound – 450 gm) pork
   and beans

Fry bacon in skillet until crisp. Remove from skillet, crumble. Pour off all but 2 to 3 tablespoons (30 to 45 ml) fat. Add onion and green pepper and saute until tender. Add remaining ingredients and mix lightly. Spoon into a buttered 6 cup (1.44 L) casserole and bake at 350°F (175°C) for 30 minutes.

PANBROILED CANADIAN—STYLE BACON
WITH CRUSHED PINEAPPLE

This makes a nice lunch. Start with tomato juice.

1 pound (0.45 kg) Canadian-style
  bacon, cut in thin slices
2 – 3 teaspoons (5 to 15 ml)
  bacon fat

2 tablespoons (30 ml) flour
1 can (15½ ounce – 439 gm)
  crushed pineapple
4 slices toasted whole wheat bread

Panbroil bacon in bacon fat, turning to brown both sides, about 6 minutes. Remove from pan and keep warm. Add flour to fat in pan and mix well. Add pineapple and its juice to flour mixture and cook and stir until heated through. To serve, spoon pineapple onto toast cut in triangles and top with bacon slices. Makes 4 servings.

BAKED CANADIAN-STYLE BACON

Bake some sweet potatoes while bacon is in the oven and a casserole of mixed vegetables.

1 whole Canadian-style bacon,
  2 to 4 pounds (896 – 1792 gm)
½ cup (125 ml) brown sugar

½ teaspoon (2 ml) dry mustard
1 to 2 tablespoons (15 to 30 ml)
  vinegar

Remove casing from bacon and put on rack in pan. Combine brown sugar, mustard and vinegar. Spread over bacon. Bake at 325°F (160°C) for 30 minutes per pound or 1 – 2 hours. Baste with brown sugar sauce and pan drippings during baking. Makes 6 to 12 servings.

Protein, of which meat is an excellent source, is a necessary nutrient, essential to growth and life.

This is a Chef-type salad. Crusty French rolls go well with it.

2 quarts (1 10 ounce − 280 gm)
   package fresh spinach
4 hard cooked eggs
1 can (16 ounce − 448 gm) chop
   suey vegetables, drained
6 slices bacon

¼ cup (50 ml) finely chopped onion
¼ cup (50 ml) vinegar
2 teaspoons (10 ml) Worcestershire sauce
1 teaspoon (5 ml) salt
Fresh ground pepper to taste

Wash spinach well and drain. Cut off stems and cut leaves coarsely. Peel and slice eggs. Combine spinach, eggs and chop suey vegetables in a large bowl.

Dice bacon and saute in skillet until crisp. Remove from skillet and reserve. Add onion and cook 2 to 3 minutes, until soft, but not browned. Remove skillet from heat and add vinegar, Worcestershire sauce, salt and pepper. Toss with bacon and spinach mixture. Serve at once. Makes 4 generous luncheon size servings.

Reduce peeking into ovens and refrigerators.

CHICKEN A LA EVERYTHING

How to Buy

Chicken is merchandised today so that there are any number of choices you can make when you go to purchase it.

There are: **Whole chickens** — 2½–3 pounds (1.125–1.35 kg) which are called broiler-fryers. These young chickens are so tender that they can be cooked by direct heat. They can be roasted whole, if one wishes, but are more likely cut into quarters or halves for broiling or disjointed for frying.

Roasters — run up to 5 pounds (2.25 kg) and make fine roast chicken, cooked whole. They can also be disjointed and used for dishes where they will be braised in a sauce.

Fowl — may not be larger than a roaster, but they are older and more tough and should always be cooked by moist heat. They are perfect for dishes such as chicken and dumplings or chicken and noodles, and when "stewed" with seasonings and chilled, the meat is fine for sandwiches, salads or casseroles.

Capon — a desexed male chicken, young, weighing 4 or more pounds (1.8 kg), very tender, well meated and likely to have more fat and much in demand for roast chicken.

Quick-frozen — chicken can also be purchased in packages. The package will indicate the kinds of pieces which it contains. Chickens purchased already frozen should be stored immediately at 0°F (−18°C) when brought home unless they are to be defrosted for use at once.

In buying chicken look for uniformly fresh smooth skin, fully fleshed and meaty chicken. If the bird wears the USDA "Grade A" inspection shield, that is a certification that it has been produced under high quality conditions, supervised by the USDA and has their best grade. Young birds have a flexible breast bone, thin skin and evidence of pin feathers. The skin is pale. Older birds have more color in their skin, verging on yellow and their skin is more rough.

Besides these general classifications chicken can be purchased whole, split, cut up — by a single chicken, in family packs with giblets or without, in packages of legs, legs and thighs, breasts boned or with bone, breasts with wings, wings alone, giblets, livers and packages of necks and backs. So you see you can buy practically anything you may need or want.

How to Care for Chicken

Chicken is very fragile and should be brought home at once from the market and stored in the coldest part of the refrigerator. Store-packaged chicken should be removed from package, giblets, if any, removed (store separately) and chicken washed and dried. Wrap it loosely in wax paper and keep no longer than 1 or 2 days. After that it should be cooked or frozen. It can be frozen in the manner in which you wish to use it, i.e., quartered or halved for broiling or cut-up for frying or whole. Wrap the individual pieces in plastic wrap for easy separation during defrosting. Then overwrap in moisture, vapor-resistant aluminum foil or polyethylene wrap. Seal, label, date.

STORAGE TIMES FOR CHICKEN

Raw Chicken	If frozen at 0°F (-18°C)
Whole chickens	12 months
Chicken pieces	9 months
Giblets	3 months
Chicken livers	3 months

Cooked Chicken	
Pieces covered with broth	6 months
Pieces not covered with broth	1 month
Cooked chicken dishes	6 months
Fried chicken	4 months

Cooking frozen chicken

It is best to defrost chicken completely before cooking, and the best way to do it is in the refrigerator. If you get caught short of time to defrost, chicken in a waterproof package can be submerged in cold water to hurry defrosting. Change water often.

Timetable for defrosting frozen chicken in refrigerator

4 pounds (1.8 kg) and over	1 to 1½ days
Less than 4 pounds (1.8 kg)	12 to 16 hours

(Broiler — Fryer — Roaster or Capon)

Chicken may be roasted with or without stuffing. If roasted without stuffing reduce the cooking time.

1 chicken for roasting 3 to 5 pounds (1.35 – 2.25 kg)
Salt and fresh ground pepper
Butter or margarine for basting

Stuffing:

½ cup (125 ml) butter or margarine

4 tablespoons (60 ml) finely chopped onion

4 tablespoons (60 ml) finely chopped celery

4 cups (1000 ml) bread cubes
½ teaspoon (2 ml) salt
½ teaspoon (2 ml) dried thyme
½ teaspoon (2 ml) dried sage
½ teaspoon (2 ml) poultry seasoning

Melt butter in skillet and saute onion and celery until tender but not browned. Add remaining ingredients and continue cooking and stirring until bread cubes are lightly browned and flavors blended. Makes enough stuffing for a 4 pound (1.8 kg) chicken.

To Roast:

Wash chicken inside and out with running water. Pat dry. Rub inside and out with salt and pepper. Prepare stuffing as directed and stuff neck and body cavity of chicken. Secure neck cavity by reversing wings under back so as to hold neck skin over stuffing. Skewer or tie legs and body cavity. Brush chicken with melted butter. Place on rack in roasting pan. Roast at 350°F (175°C) for about 30 minutes per pound. Check for doneness by feeling leg joint. If the flesh feels soft and the joint moves easily it is done. Baste chicken during roasting.

Other stuffings:

Sausage Stuffing

½ pound (0.224 kg) pork sausage
½ cup (125 ml) finely chopped celery

½ cup (125 ml) finely chopped onion
4 cups (1000 ml) bread cubes

Cook sausage and vegetables over moderate heat until sausage is done. Add bread and continue cooking and stirring until bread cubes are lightly browned and blended with sausage. Enough for a 4 pound (1.8 kg) chicken.

Rice and Apricot Stuffing

6 tablespoons (90 ml) butter or
  margarine
3 tablespoons (45 ml) finely
  chopped onion
1 tablespoon (15 ml) chopped parsley
⅔ cup (160 ml) finely chopped celery

2½ cups (625 ml) cooked rice
½ cup (125 ml) dried apricots,
  cut in small pieces
½ teaspoon (2 ml) poultry
  seasoning

Heat butter in skillet and saute onion, parsley and celery until tender. Stir in remaining ingredients. Enough for a 4 pound (1.8 kg) chicken.

MEAT STUFFING FOR CHICKEN

---

2 tablespoons (30 ml) oil
¾ pound (0.3375 kg) ground beef
1 cup (250 ml) cooked rice
¼ cup (50 ml) chopped blanched
  almonds

1 teaspoon (5 ml) salt
Fresh ground pepper to taste
¼ teaspoon (1 ml) cinnamon
½ cup (125 ml) water
2 tablespoons (30 ml) lemon juice

Heat oil in large skillet. Add beef and cook and stir until lightly browned. Add remaining ingredients, blending well. Cover and simmer about 15 minutes or until all liquid is absorbed. Use as a stuffing for neck and body cavity of roaster. Makes enough for a 4 pound (1.8 kg) roaster.

Turn off the oven for the last ten minutes' cooking time (in the case of anything but souffle and cake baking) to let the food finish cooking on residual heat.

BROILED CHICKEN

Broiler — fryer chickens from 1½ to 2½ pounds (0.675 – 1.125 kg) are the best size for broiling. The 1½ pound (0.675 kg) chickens should be split, the larger size quartered for broiling. Wash the chickens and dry. Place on broiler rack and brush with softened butter, margarine or oil. Season with salt and fresh ground pepper to taste, or use seasoned salts such as celery, garlic, onion or mixed seasonings. Place under broiler about 4-inches (10 cm) from source of heat and broil 30 minutes, turning once. Brush with butter when chicken is turned.

VARIATIONS

Barbecue sauce: ½ cup (125 ml) catsup, ½ cup (125 ml) oil, ¼ cup (50 ml) brown sugar, 2 tablespoons (30 ml) prepared mustard, ¼ cup (50 ml) vinegar, 1 teaspoon (5 ml) onion salt. Mix all ingredients well. Marinate chicken in sauce for several hours. Brush with sauce during broiling.

Oriental: ½ cup (125 ml) oil, ¼ cup (50 ml) soy sauce, ¼ cup (50 ml) lemon juice, ¼ cup (50 ml) honey, 3 teaspoons (15 ml) grated onion. Mix all ingredients well. Marinate chicken in sauce for several hours. Brush with sauce during broiling.

Lemon chicken: Allow ½ lemon for each whole broiler. Rub and squeeze juice from lemon on chicken. Sprinkle with salt and fresh ground pepper. Let stand 30 minutes. Brush chicken with melted butter or margarine and sprinkle with paprika and broil as directed.

Italian: 1 envelope (⅝ ounce – 17.5 gm) Italian salad dressing mix, ½ cup (125 ml) melted butter or margarine, 3 tablespoons (45 ml) lime juice. Combine all ingredients. Brush chicken with dressing mixture. Broil as directed

Sherry: ½ cup (125 ml) melted butter or margarine, ½ cup (125 ml) dry sherry, 2 tablespoons (30 ml) soy sauce, 2 tablespoons (30 ml) lemon juice, 1 teaspoon (5 ml) fresh ground ginger. Combine all ingredients. Brush chicken with mixture. Broil as directed.

PAN FRIED CHICKEN

There are as many ways to pan fry chicken as there are cooks, I think. My great aunt Mary, who was a famed cook in the small town where I was born, did not believe in dipping chicken in flour because she wanted the skin browned — not the flour. So she fried chicken unadorned in half lard and half butter. And it tasted pretty special to a young girl. Very often I fry it that way, though just as often I dip it in seasoned flour. Then there are those who use crumbs and batter. So like many things in cooking, one chooses one's favorite method and learns not to argue the merits. Today's chickens are so tender they can be fried the open pan method without putting a lid on the skillet. When frying chicken, I freeze the boney pieces and soon accumulate enough for a good chicken soup.

Method 1.

Choose a chicken about 2½ to 3½ pounds (1.125 – 1.575 kg) and cut up or buy chicken parts. Allow ¾ pound (0.3375 kg) per person. Save the boney pieces like the back and neck for soup. Wash and dry pieces. Mix ¼ cup (50 ml) flour with 1 teaspoon (5 ml) salt and fresh ground pepper to taste. Heat enough half lard (or soft shortening) and half butter or margarine in a large skillet to make about ½-inch (1.25 cm) deep when melted. Heat over moderately high unit and brown chicken. (Do not crowd pieces. Use two skillets if necessary). Reduce heat and continue cooking chicken 20 to 30 minutes or until tender, turning pieces often with tongs.

Method 2.

Wash and dry chicken very well. Fry as above. Season with salt and fresh ground pepper when chicken is cooked. This unadorned chicken has a tendency to stick to the skillet if not well dried.

Method 3.

Wash and dry chicken. Mix 2 eggs with 2 tablespoons (30 ml) water and 1 teaspoon (5 ml) salt. Dip chicken pieces in egg mixture and then in flour. Let stand at room temperature 15 – 20 minutes before frying. Fry 3 to 4 pieces at a time at 350°F (175°C) in deep fat or oil for about 15 minutes or until browned well. Drain on paper towels.

Method 4.

Cover chicken with milk and let stand 1 hour. Beat 2 eggs with 2 tablespoons (30 ml) milk or water. Dip chicken in egg mixture, then in mixture of ¾ cup (180 ml) flour, ¾ cup (180 ml) cracker crumbs, 2 teaspoons (10 ml) paprika, 1 teaspoon (5 ml) salt and fresh ground pepper to taste. Let chicken stand at room temperature 15 – 20 minutes, then fry as directed in Method 3.

Method 5.

Wash chicken and dry. Make a batter by mixing together 1 cup (250 ml) flour, ½ teaspoon (2 ml) salt, 1 beaten egg, 1 cup (250 ml) milk and 1 tablespoon (15 ml) oil. Dip chicken pieces in batter and fry at once as in Method 3.

Note: Many homemakers flour chicken by putting the seasoned flour in a bag and adding the chicken pieces a few at a time and shaking to cover with flour. If any seasoned flour is left it can be used for gravy.

OVEN FRIED CHICKEN

Oven frying of chicken is a very neat way to prepare it. It requires little watching and a whole meal can be cooked in the oven at the same time. Bake potatoes to serve with sour cream and chives and a grapefruit-cranberry salad.

Classic Oven Fried Chicken

1 broiler-fryer, 2½ to 3 pounds
   (1.125 – 1.35 kg)
½ cup (125 ml) evaporated milk
1 cup (250 ml) cornflake crumbs

1 teaspoon (5 ml) salt
½ teaspoon (2 ml) paprika
Fresh ground pepper to taste

Cut up chicken and wash and dry pieces. (Save boney pieces for soup). Dip chicken in evaporated milk and then in cornflake crumbs which have been mixed with salt, paprika and pepper. Line a shallow baking dish with aluminum foil and lay chicken pieces in pan being careful that they do not touch. Bake at 350°F (175°C) for 1 hour or until chicken is tender. Makes 4 servings.

OVEN FRIED CHICKEN — PLAIN

Put a pan of potato slices dipped in butter and a casserole of green beans in the oven.

1 broiler – fryer 2½ – 3 pounds
   (1.125 – 1.35 kg)
¼ cup (50 ml) flour
½ teaspoon (2 ml) salt
½ teaspoon (2 ml) poultry seasoning

½ teaspoon (2 ml) paprika
Fresh ground pepper to taste
¼ cup (50 ml) melted butter or
   margarine

Cut up chicken and wash and dry. Mix flour with seasonings and dip chicken pieces in flour. Place skin side up in a buttered baking pan. Drizzle melted butter over chicken. Bake at 350°F (175°C) for 1 hour or until tender and brown. Makes 4 servings.

CHICKEN WITH GRAPEFRUIT

Serve with the thin noodles, fresh green beans

1 broiler — fryer 2½ – 3 pounds,
   cut up (1.125 – 1.35 kg)
4 tablespoons (60 ml) butter or
   margarine
½ teaspoon (2 ml) salt
Fresh ground pepper to taste

1 grapefruit
½ cup (125 ml) whole cranberry
   sauce
1 tablespoon (15 ml) honey
⅛ teaspoon (0.55 cm) ground
   cloves

Cut up chicken, saving boney pieces for broth. Heat butter in skillet and brown chicken pieces on all sides. Place in a flat, buttered casserole as browned. Season with salt and pepper.

Peel grapefruit, remove sections and squeeze juice from pulp into skillet in which chicken was fried. Add cranberry sauce, honey and cloves and heat, scraping brown crust from skillet. Add grapefruit sections. Spoon sauce over chicken and bake at 350°F (175°C) for 45 minutes or until tender, basting several times with sauce in casserole. Makes 4 servings.

CHICKEN VALENCIA

Serve with steamed rice, Spanish salad

1 roaster chicken, about 5 pounds
   (2.25 kg)
3 tablespoons (45 ml) diced
   salt pork
¼ cup (50 ml) oil
1 teaspoon (5 ml) salt
1 can (16 ounce (448 gm) tomato
   sauce

2 cups (0.48 L) dry white wine
8 small white onions, peeled
2 carrots, peeled, cut in pieces
¼ cup (50 ml) sliced pepperoni
   or Keilbasa sausage
Salt and fresh ground pepper
   to taste

Cut chicken into serving pieces. Wash and dry. Fry salt pork over medium heat until crisp in large skillet or Dutch oven. Remove salt pork and reserve. Add oil to skillet and brown chicken pieces. Pour off any oil in skillet. Combine remaining ingredients (except salt pork) and simmer, covered, until chicken is tender, about 50 minutes. Sprinkle with salt pork. Makes 6 to 8 servings.

CHICKEN ORLANDO

Noodles and sauteed cherry tomatoes would make the menu complete.

2 broiler — fryers, 2½ pounds
  (1.125 kg) each
2 cups (500 ml) bread crumbs
¼ cup (50 ml) chopped parsley
1 clove garlic, crushed
2 teaspoons (10 ml) salt

Fresh ground pepper to taste
1 teaspoon (5 ml) paprika
½ cup (125 ml) grated Parmesan
  cheese
¾ cup (180 ml) melted butter
  or margarine

Cut up chickens. (Save bony pieces for soup.) Wash and dry. Mix bread crumbs with parsley, seasonings and cheese. Dip each piece of chicken into butter, then crumbs. Place pieces skin side up on a shallow buttered baking pan. Sprinkle remaining crumbs and butter over chicken in pan. Bake at 350°F (175°C) for 1 hour or until chicken is tender. Baste with pan juices and/or additional butter from time to time during baking. Makes 6 servings.

CURRIED CHICKEN MOUSSE

A lovely luncheon dish. Serve thin white bread sandwiches and chutney relish with this Mousse.

2 envelopes unflavored gelatin
2 cups (500 ml) chicken broth
3 tablespoons (45 ml) lemon juice
1 teaspoon (5 ml) dry mustard
2 teaspoons (10 ml) curry powder
1 teaspoon (5 ml) onion salt

1 cup (250 ml) finely diced celery
2 cups (500 ml) dairy sour cream
3 cups (750 ml) finely diced
  chicken
¼ cup (50 ml) finely diced
  almonds
Lettuce, cherry tomatoes

Soften gelatin in ½ cup (125 ml) cold chicken broth. Heat remaining broth, add to gelatin and stir until gelatin is dissolved. Mix in lemon juice and seasonings. Taste and add salt if needed. Chill in refrigerator until mixture begins to thicken. Fold in sour cream, mixing well. Stir in chicken and almonds. Spoon in a 1½ quart (1.425 L) mold. Chill until firm. Unmold on platter. Garnish with lettuce and cherry tomatoes. Makes 6 servings.

PER'S CHICKEN

Parslied potatoes and celery and peas with a pineapple salad complete the meal.

4 chicken breasts, boned
1 egg, beaten
1 teaspoon (5 ml) prepared
    mustard
1 teaspoon (5 ml) salt

1 tablespoon (15 ml) Worcester-
    shire sauce
Dash Tabasco
¾ cup (180 ml) Italian flavored
    bread crumbs

Wash and dry chicken breasts and cut in half. Dip in egg mixed with mustard, salt, Worcestershire sauce and Tabasco, then in seasoned crumbs. Place in a buttered shallow baking dish and bake at 350°F (175°C) for 1 hour or until tender. Makes 4 to 6 servings.

CHICKEN LUCILLE

Brown rice and green lima beans with a tossed salad are the menu.

2 broiler — fryers, about 3 pounds
    (1.35 kg)
¼ cup (50 ml) flour
1 teaspoon (5 ml) salt
Fresh ground pepper to taste
¼ cup (50 ml) butter or
    margarine
¾ cup (180 ml) catsup

¾ cup (180 ml) dry sherry wine
¼ cup (50 ml) water
2½ tablespoons (37.5 ml)
    lemon juice
2 teaspoons (10 ml) Worcester-
    shire sauce
¾ cup (180 ml) chopped onion
½ teaspoon (2 ml) dried rosemary

Cut up chicken and wash and dry pieces. Save boney pieces for soup. Mix flour with salt and pepper and sprinkle over chicken. Heat butter in skillet and brown chicken on all sides. As browned, transfer to a buttered 2-quart (2.375 L) casserole. When chicken is all browned, add remaining ingredients to skillet and cook and scrape crust from bottom of skillet. Pour over chicken in casserole. Cover and bake at 325°F (160°C) until tender. Makes 6 servings.

HERBED CHICKEN BREASTS IN GRAVY

Serve mashed potatoes and buttered carrots and grapefruit salad.

3 whole chicken breasts
1 cup (250 ml) dairy sour cream
1 teaspoon (5 ml) salt
Fresh ground pepper to taste

1½ cups (375 ml) packaged herb-
seasoned bread stuffing mix, crushed
1 can (10½ ounce – 294 gm) condensed
cream of mushroom soup
½ cup (125 ml) milk

Split chicken breasts. Cover with sour cream and marinate over night in the refrigerator. Remove from marinade (reserve sour cream), sprinkle with salt and pepper and roll in finely crushed stuffing mix. Place chicken breasts in a buttered shallow baking dish skin side down. Bake at 350°F (175°C) for 30 minutes. Turn pieces and bake 30 minutes longer or until tender. Combine soup with milk and sour cream and heat. Serve with chicken. Makes 6 servings.

COQ AU VIN

A classic French dish for chicken. Parslied potatoes and a tossed salad can accompany it.

2 broiler — fryers, about 2 pounds
each (.90 kg)
¼ cup (50 ml) diced salt pork
1 clove garlic, finely diced
4 shallots, chopped
¼ cup (50 ml) chopped yellow
onion
¼ teaspoon (1 ml) thyme

12 small white onions, peeled
1 cup small whole mushrooms
2 cups (500 ml) dry red wine
1 teaspoon (5 ml) salt
Fresh ground pepper to taste

Cut up chickens. Save boney pieces for soup. Wash and dry. Fry salt pork until lightly browned. Push to one side and brown chicken pieces. Add garlic, shallots and chopped onion and brown lightly. Add remaining ingredients and bring to a boil. Simmer, covered, for 30 to 40 minutes, until chicken is tender. Makes 6 servings.

CHICKEN LIVERS WITH PINEAPPLE

Serve this sweet-sour chicken liver recipe over hot rice — add green beans and tomato and cottage cheese salad.

1 pound (0.45 kg) chicken livers
¼ cup (50 ml) soy sauce
¼ cup (50 ml) oil
1 can (8¼ ounce − 234 gm)
   pineapple chunks, drained
½ cup (125 ml) blanched almonds,
   slivered and toasted

1¼ cups (300 ml) pineapple
   juice and water
2 tablespoons (30 ml) lemon juice
¼ teaspoon (1 ml) salt
¼ cup (50 ml) sugar
2 tablespoons (30 ml) cornstarch

Wash and drain chicken livers. Cut each liver in half and dip in soy sauce. Heat oil in skillet and quickly brown livers. Add pineapple chunks and almonds and remove from heat. Combine pineapple juice and remaining ingredients in a saucepan and bring to a boil, stirring, until sauce boils and is thickened and clear. Combine with chicken livers and bring again to the boil. Makes 6 servings.

STEWED CHICKEN AND NOODLES

Green peas and cranberry sauce go well with this old-fashioned dish.

1 fowl, about 5 pounds (2.25 kg)
1 lemon
1 medium onion
1 rib celery
1 carrot, peeled

1 teaspoon (5 ml) salt
6 whole peppercorns
1 bay leaf
1 pound (0.45 kg) medium noodles

Wash fowl and rub with cut lemon. Put in a large saucepan. Add onion, celery, carrot, salt, peppercorns and bay leaf. Bring to a boil and simmer about 3 hours or until tender. Cool in broth. When cool enough to handle, remove meat from bone in as large pieces as possible. Strain broth. Bring broth to a boil and cook noodles in it 9 minutes or until tender. Strain noodles from broth and thicken broth with a small amount of flour. Reheat chicken in broth. Serve chicken and noodles with gravy. Makes 6 servings.

Note: This recipe for stewed chicken can be used for chicken salad or scalloped chicken. Cool chicken in broth, remove meat from bones and chill. Strain broth and use at once to make chicken noodle or rice or vegetable soup, or freeze for future use.

FUN 'N FANCY COOKING

NOW THAT'S ENTERTAINMENT

Entertaining can be anything from a spur of the moment coffee break at 10 o'clock in the morning to a light supper at midnight after the theater.

Whether the party is for 2 or 22, if it isn't spontaneous, the best way to make it a success is to plan ahead. Put it on paper so that no detail is overlooked.

Unless someone is invited for "pot luck" at the last moment, most parties are scheduled far enough in advance so that the major share of the work can be done far ahead. The less last minute work, the more you will be free to enjoy the party.

I knew a hostess who tried to plan her yearly entertaining within a close enough span so that when she cleaned the silver and washed the goblets for the first party they would be in good shape for the next 3 or 4 parties to be given. Today's hosts and hostesses are frequently working outside their home, and need to find as many short cuts as they can.

Plan menus where as much of the food as possible can be prepared in advance. With efficient freezers we can cook ahead for the freezer to have homemade bread, vegetables and meats ready to use. Delectable desserts and hors d'ouevres can also be frozen ahead of time.

Buffet service is the most practical service without assistance. The food can be set on a buffet or table, the guests help themselves and are seated at the dining room table, or small tables set in the living room, and in some homes, on the floor. It is also practical because guests can help themselves to as much or as little as they want to eat without embarrassment.

Let everyone join in the preparing and serving, and the party will be remembered as a good time had by all.

Beef and Mushroom Ragout has all the qualities of a good main dish for a party. Easy on the hostess because it can be all (or partly) prepared the day before. The menu might go like this:

Hors d'ouevres with pre-dinner beverage

Beef and Mushroom Ragout (p. 48)

Buttered Noodles

Bowl of Vegetable Relish
(which could have gone from the pre-dinner beverage to the buffet table)

Buttered Hot Rolls

Angel Pie

106

The schedule:

- Prepare Beef and Mushroom Ragout the day ahead and refrigerate. Reheat on low heat 30 to 40 minutes, or in the oven.
- Noodles can be cooked early on, mixed with butter and reheated in the oven in the casserole in which they will be served while the rolls are heating.
- The rolls would have been made or bought and frozen weeks before the dinner.
- Vegetable relishes can be prepared the day ahead of the party and kept in closed plastic bags with a few ice cubes tucked in the zag when the relishes are put in.
- Angel pie is made and frozen any time ahead up to 6 weeks.

Set up the buffet:

- Serve Ragout in a chafing dish.
- Have noodles in casserole and rolls in basket on a hot tray.
- Fresh relishes in a bowl to be served as finger food.
- Dinner beverage should be on the dinner table (unless coffee is served with dinner and then it is poured after guests are seated).

Perhaps a friend will help clear the tables and serve dessert and coffee. Or if buffet service is preferred for dessert, have buffet cleared of dinner foods and dessert and coffee service put on when all the guests have served themselves. (Angel Pie should be out of the freezer at least 30 minutes before it is cut) While guests are helping themselves to dessert someone can be clearing the tables.

This simple pattern gives an idea for one dinner. Other recipes can be slipped into the pattern for easy entertaining.

It is a smart idea to keep track of the menu (including the kinds of hors d'ouevres served) and the name of the guests for each party along with the date. This helps keep your menus varied and more interesting if you have many of the same guests from time to time.

Here are a selection of hors d'ouevres recipes hot and cold, to further help you with your entertaining ways.

Make Any Number:

Barber Poles

Spread sesame-seed bread sticks with softened cream cheese wrap thin sliced ham around each. Chill.

Beef Lover

Dice cold cooked beef very fine. Season with lime juice, Tabasco sauce and onion salt. Pile on slices of party rye, toasted and buttered.

Kippers in Bacon

Cut kippered herring crosswise into 1-inch (2.5 cm) pieces. Sprinkle with lemon juice. Wrap each piece with a half slice of bacon. Fasten with toothpick. Broil until bacon is crisp. Serve hot.

Hot Bites

Cut frankfurters in 4 or 5 pieces crosswise. Dip in catsup and roll in crushed cornflakes. Place on a greased baking sheet and bake at 400°F. (200°C) for 10 to 15 minutes.

Bacon Cracker Teaser

Cut bacon in half crosswise and wrap half slice around square soda cracker. Place on a greased baking sheet and bake at 375°F. (190°C) for 20 minutes or until bacon is crisp.

COCKTAIL MEATBALLS

1 pound (0.45 kg) ground beef
⅓ cup (80 ml) finely chopped water
  chestnuts
2 green onions, finely chopped
¼ teaspoon (1 ml) freshly grated or
  ground ginger.

3 tablespoons (45 ml) soy sauce
2 tablespoons (30 ml) water
Fresh ground black pepper to taste
2 tablespoons (30 ml) oil

Blend meat lightly with chestnuts, onions, seasonings and water. Shape into bite-sized meat balls. Chill in freezer 1 hour. Heat oil in skillet and brown meat balls on all sides. Serve in a chafing dish with toothpicks. Makes 12 servings.

CRISPY MEAT BALLS

1 pound (0.45 kg) top round steak,
  ground twice
1 teaspoon (5 ml) salt
½ teaspoon (2 ml) fresh ground
  pepper
½ teaspoon (2 ml) thick steak
  sauce

½ cup (125 ml) canned potato sticks
½ cup (125 ml) canned French fried
  onions
½ cup (125 ml) finely chopped fresh
  parsley

This is one of the times when you might want to grind the beef yourself. Mix it lightly with salt, pepper and thick steak sauce. Chop potato sticks and onions very fine and mix with parsley. Shape meat mixture into 50 to 60 small balls and roll in potato onion mixture. Chill. Serve with picks.

CRANBERRY MEAT BALLS

1 pound (0.45 kg) ground beef
½ cup (125 ml) dry bread crumbs
1 egg
3 tablespoons (45 ml) chopped onion
1 teaspoon (5 ml) salt
Fresh ground pepper to taste

2 tablespoons (30 ml) water
2 tablespoons (30 ml) butter or
  margarine
1 cup (250 ml) jellied cranberry sauce
1 can (8 ounce − 227 gm) tomato sauce
½ cup (125 ml) water
1 tablespoon (15 ml) horseradish

Mix ground beef with bread crumbs, egg, onion, salt, pepper and 2 tablespoons (15 ml) water. Shape into about 25 small meat balls. Place on cookie sheet and chill in the freezer 1 hour. Brown quickly in butter turning to brown all over. Pour off excess fat. Mix cranberry with tomato sauce, ½ cup (125 ml) water and horseradish. Pour over meatballs in skillet. Bring to a boil and cover and simmer over low heat 25 to 30 minutes. Serve hot with sauce.

CHICKEN CANAPES

2 cups (500 ml) finely diced
  cooked chicken
¼ cup (50 ml) chopped almonds
½ cup (125 ml) mayonnaise

Salt to taste
12 slices thin sliced white
  bread
Butter or margarine

Mix chicken with almonds, mayonnaise and salt. Remove crusts from bread and spread lightly with butter. Spread with filling and cut each slice into 3 finger length pieces. Garnish with grated egg yolk, chopped parsley or thinly sliced olives. Makes 36.

DEVILED HAM ROUNDS

1 (2 crust package) pastry mix
1 can (2½ ounce — 60 gm)
  deviled ham

2 to 3 tablespoons white wine
Sesame seed

Mix pastry with ham and wine. Roll ½-inch thick on a floured board. Cut into small rounds. Sprinkle with sesame seeds. Bake on a baking sheet at 450°F. (230°C) 8 to 10 minutes or until lightly browned. Makes 36.

BEEF JERKY

A popular party snack

1½ – 2-inch (3.75 – 5 cm) thick
   boneless sirloin steak
   (2 pounds (0.9 kg))

Seasoned salt
Fresh ground pepper to taste

    Remove the fat from steak and partially freeze by leaving in freezer 1 to 2 hours. With a sharp knife cut into very thin strips. Sprinkle with seasoned salt and pepper. Hang over cake racks and dry in oven at 150°F (65°C) for 5 to 6 hours. Leave oven door open slightly during this time. Store jerky in a tightly covered container. Serves about 50.

HAM PATÉ

1 teaspoon (5 ml) unflavored gelatin
½ cup (125 ml) cold water
1 cup (250 ml) diced cooked ham
1 teaspoon (5 ml) prepared mustard

1 tablespoon (15 ml) horseradish
1 teaspoon (5 ml) Worcestershire sauce
1 teaspoon (5 ml) grated onion

    Combine gelatin with water. When softened, heat until gelatin is dissolved. Cool. Combine in blender with remaining ingredients. Blend until smooth. Spoon into a 1½ cup (375 ml) mold. Chill until firm. Unmold on platter and serve with crackers.

HAM CRUNCH

1 cup (250 ml) ground cooked ham
2 tablespoons (30 ml) Worcestershire
   sauce
2 tablespoons (30 ml) prepared mustard

¼ cup (50 ml) mayonnaise
2 tablespoons (30 ml) pickle relish
2 tablespoons (30 ml) finely chopped
   celery

    Mix all ingredients and chill well. Use as a spread on squares of buttered rye bread. Makes 1 cup (250 ml).

PEANUT BUTTER BACON SQUARES

4 slices bacon
⅔ cup (160 ml) crunchy peanut
butter
1 package (3 ounce − 84 gm) cream
cheese

6 to 8 tablespoons (90 to 120 ml)
sherry wine
⅛ teaspoon (0.5 − ml) dried
rosemary
12 slices bread

Cook bacon until crisp. Drain on paper towels and crumble. Have peanut butter and cream cheese at room temperature and mix with wine and rosemary until blended. Fold in crumbled bacon. Toast slices of bread on one side. Spread untoasted side with peanut butter mixture. Cut each slice in 4 squares. Broil until hot and bubbly. Serve hot. Makes 48.

TASTY RIB FINGERS

2 pounds (0.9 kg) spareribs
1 tablespoon (15 ml) butter or
margarine
3 tablespoons (45 ml) chopped onion
1 ½ tablespoons (22 ml) brown sugar
1 tablespoon (15 ml) Worcestershire
sauce

2 tablespoons (30 ml) lemon juice
1½ tablespoons (22 ml) vinegar
⅓ cup (80 ml) water
⅔ cup (160 ml) chili sauce
½ teaspoon (2 ml) salt

Have meat man crack spareribs into about 2-inch (5 cm) lengths. Cut between ribs into individual pieces. Place in a shallow pan and bake at 400°F (200°C) 15 minutes. Pour off fat.

Heat butter in small saucepan and saute onion until tender. Add remaining ingredients and simmer 10 minutes, covered. Pour over ribs in pan and bake 45 minutes longer or until browned and crispy. Serve hot or cold. Serves about 30.

SASSY SAUSAGE

8 pork sausage links
5 tablespoons (75 ml) brown sugar
5 tablespoons (75 ml) rum

5 tablespoons (75 ml) soy sauce
1 tablespoon (15 ml) orange
marmalade

Cut each sausage into 4 or 5 pieces crosswise. Cook in skillet over low heat until lightly browned. Pour off fat. Mix remaining ingredients and pour over sausage. Simmer 10 minutes. Serve hot with picks. Makes 32 or 40.

HAWAIIAN CHICKEN PUFFS

1 cup (250 ml) finely chopped
  cooked chicken
⅓ cup (80 ml) finely chopped
  Macadamia nuts
2 green onions, finely chopped
⅓ cup (80 ml) mayonnaise
White pepper to taste

¼ teaspoon (1 ml) lemon juice
⅛ teaspoon (0.5 ml) ground
  nutmeg
15 round butter crackers (about)
Paprika

Mix chicken with nuts and remaining ingredients except crackers, blending well. Mound spoonfuls on crackers. Sprinkle with paprika. Brown under broiler about 5 minutes. Makes approximately 16.

CHICKEN LITTLE

1 cup (250 ml) diced cooked chicken
1 stalk celery
¼ cup (50 ml) pecans
4 tablespoons (60 ml) mayonnaise

½ teaspoon (2 ml) curry powder
¼ teaspoon (1 ml) salt
1 tablespoon (15 ml) sherry wine

Put chicken, celery and pecans through grinder or chop up in the blender. Add remaining ingredients and mix well. Use as a spread for crackers or buttered bread rounds. Makes about 1¼ cups (300 ml).

CORNUCOPIAS

1 package (3 ounce − 84 gm) cream
  cheese
1 to 2 tablespoons (15 to 30 ml)
  cream
½ teaspoon (2 ml) horseradish

¼ teaspoon (1 ml) onion salt
½ teaspoon (2 ml) prepared mustard
6 to 8 thin slices small bologna or
  salami

Soften cream cheese and blend with cream, horseradish, onion salt and mustard. Remove rind from meat if any. Cut slices in half. Spread with cheese and roll to shape like a cornucopia. Fasten with toothpick. Place in dish and cover. Chill. Makes about 1 dozen.

No Pickle in the Middle

Cut ¼ inch (0.625 cm) thick slices of bologna to fit thin slices of dill pickle. Sandwich a slice of bologna between 2 pickle slices. Spear on a toothpick to serve.

SUMMER 'N SMOKE COOKING ALL YEAR ROUND

Barbecuing has gone from an occasional way of cooking to a regular summer thing and an enjoyable way of informal cooking and eating for the family and guests. In fact many barbecue grills including my own are so situated that they can be used anytime during the winter.

Right beside it is a cabinet where the long handled tongs, forks, electric starter and other paraphernalia is kept to make it easy to use.

Choosing a grill:

If you are a novice and not sure that you want to devote summers to outdoor cooking, it is my suggestion that you buy an inexpensive grill to start with. In fact my first was a rectangular grill with collapsible legs that could be taken in the car trunk. I've not had one that cooked better, though my present grill is larger and has a rotisserie if I wish to use it. So visit your hardware or department store and make a choice. In between the folding grill and a larger grill are hibachis, usually made from iron and built in varying sizes. The permanent fireplace grill is either indoors or outdoors.

Additional equipment needed:

Long handled tongs, fork and turner are efficient for handling food during cooking and for avoiding being too close to the heat. It's wise to have pot holders though many people prefer heat proof gloves. I keep a pair of old gloves for handling the charcoal. Salt shaker and pepper mill — a small pot and brush for spreading the barbecue sauce and a sharp knife are good additions. If it is not convenient to have a cabinet near the grill where these things can be kept permanently, keep them in a caddy or basket so they will be readily available.

Fuel:

There are gas and electric grills available if you want to do away with charcoal, but charcoal is the predominant fuel. Some people swear by hickory or fruit woods. And if you use charcoal its nice to have hickory chips and throw a few on to get the aroma and flavor.

Starting the fire:

The fire bowl can be lined with heavy duty aluminum foil, cutting vent holes as needed. If you prefer, a base of sand, gravel or vermiculite can be put into the fire bowl and on which the fire will burn. In either case, the foil enables you to take out the ashes more easily.

113

My own choice is an electric starter. A base of charcoal is laid, the starter put on and then more charcoal. In about 5−7 minutes the fire is blazing enough to unplug the starter.

Next I would choose paper and kindling and build that as a base with the briquets on top.

There are charcoal lighters, charcoal packaged in containers in which you just light the container. Again, I suggest you experiment. If you use charcoal lighting fuel, please follow the directions carefully.

Amount of charcoal:

It takes about 2 dozen briquets to make a bed of charcoal coals to cook the average dinner. Most beginners use too much charcoal.

Timing:

Anywhere from 20−30 minutes before you are ready to cook, start the fire. The charcoal should be white ash with a red center and the coals should be separated so that they are about an inch apart and the bed of coals about an inch larger than the piece of meat to be cooked.

What to Charcoal:

Steaks, ground beef, frankfurters, pork chops, ham steaks, kabobs, to name a few. The variety goes from the most expensive to the relatively cheap.

This general chart will give you an idea of timing. If you are new at it, the best way to tell whether the steak is sufficiently done or not is to cut into the center and look.

Steaks	Distance from Coals	Time — minutes
1″ (2.5 cm) thick	2 to 3 inches (5.0−7.5 cm)	15−20 rare 20−25 medium
2″ (5.00 cm) thick	3 to 5 inches (7.5−12.5 cm)	30−35 rare 40−45 medium
Ground beef patties (4 to pound (0.45 kg)	2 to 3 inches (5.0−7.5 cm)	8 med. rare
Frankfurters	2 to 3 inches (5.0−7.5 cm)	10

Convince family and friends to take more of their recreation out-of-doors.

Other suggestions:

When broiling steak trim off all the fat. It will keep fat from dripping into the fire and causing flare-up.

Porterhouse, sirloin, tenderloin, T-bone steaks can be charcoal broiled without any help from man unless a basting sauce for flavor is used.

Steaks cut from the chuck or round should be tenderized by marinating or using a meat tenderizer as directed.

Kabobs can be made of many combinations. Mushrooms, small onions, tomatoes, partially cooked chunks of sweet or white potato, pieces of green pepper, egg plant, squash, or fruit such as peaches and oranges. Any of these interspersed with cubes of beef, lamb or pork will make a tasty meal.

Turn the meat being broiled as often as practical and brush with basting sauce, if desired.

Chicken pieces or halves or quarters can be cooked over charcoal. Marinating chicken helps to keep it moist.

When using the rotisserie, be certain the meat is balanced on the rod and that the spit forks are tightened well. A meat thermometer may be used. Just see that it doesn't touch the rod or fat in the meat.

HE-MAN BURGERS

1 tablespoon (15 ml) oil
1 medium onion, finely chopped
1 clove garlic, minced
2 pounds (0.9 kg) lean ground beef
2 eggs
1 tablespoon (15 ml) chopped
   parsley

1½ teaspoons (7.5 ml) salt
Fresh ground pepper to taste
¼ cup (50 ml) Roquefort cheese
2 tablespoons (30 ml) soft
   butter
2 tablespoons (30 ml) bourbon

Heat oil in saucepan and cook onion and garlic until tender. Mix with beef, eggs, parsley, salt and pepper lightly, to blend well. Shape into 4 thick patties. With a spoon, scoop out a round hole halfway through, about the size of a silver dollar, from each patty. Mix cheese, butter and bourbon and spoon into hole. Cover with removed beef. Broil over charcoal to desired doneness. Makes 4 servings.

SOUTH AMERICAN MIXED KABOB

1 cup (250 ml) olive oil
½ cup (125 ml) lemon juice
1 garlic clove, minced
1 bay leaf

½ teaspon (2 ml) salt
2 pounds (0.9 kg) veal heart
2 pounds (0.9 kg) boneless
   sirloin steak

Combine olive oil with lemon juice, garlic, bay leaf and salt. Wash veal heart and cut out veins and arteries. Cut into 1-inch cubes. Trim fat from steak. Cut into 1-inch cubes. Stir into olive oil mixture and let marinate in refrigerator for 24 hours. String heart and beef alternately on skewers and broil over charcoal about 10 minutes, turning to brown. Makes 6 servings.

BROILED PORK CHOPS

6 rib, loin or butterfly pork chops
1 to 1½-inch (2.5 – 3.75 cm) thick
¼ cup (50 ml) melted butter
   or margarine

½ cup (125 ml) dry sherry
1 teaspoon (5 ml) dried rosemary
Salt and fresh ground pepper
   to taste

Trim fat from pork chops. Place on grill 5 inches (12.5 cm) from charcoal coals. Mix butter with sherry and rosemary. Broil chops 10 minutes on each side, brushing with sherry sauce. Continue broiling another 20 minutes, turning and brushing with sauce until pork chops are well done. Season with salt and pepper. Makes 6 servings.

HAM STEAK

2 ham steaks, 1-inch (2.5 cm)
   thick (about 2 pounds each
   (0.9 kg)
2 cups (500 ml) dry sherry

¼ cup (50 ml) melted butter
   or margarine
2 tablespoons (30 ml) dry mustard
4 tablespoons (60 ml) brown sugar

Trim fat from ham steaks. Mix remaining ingredients. Place ham steaks in a flat dish and marinate for 2 to 3 hours, turning steaks several times. Remove from marinade. Broil over charcoal about 20 minutes, turning several times and brushing with marinade during cooking. Makes 6 servings.

BARBECUED RIBS

1 cup (250 ml) condensed bouillon
1 cup (250 ml) orange marmalade
4 tablespoons (60 ml) catsup
4 tablespoons (60 ml) vinegar

2 cloves garlic, minced
1 teaspoon (5 ml) salt
Fresh ground pepper to taste
4 to 5 pounds (1.8–2.25 kg)
    country style spareribs

Combine bouillon with marmalade, catsup, vinegar, garlic, salt and pepper in saucepan. Cook and stir until marmalade is melted and mixture blended. Put spareribs in a shallow dish and cover with sauce. Refrigerate overnight or at least 8 hours. Broil over charcoal until browned and meat well done, brushing with sauce.

LAMB KABOBS

3 pounds (1.35 kg) boneless lamb
1 can (1 lb. 4 oz.–567 gm)
    pineapple chunks
2 tablespoons (30 ml) soy sauce
2 tablespoons (30 ml) lemon juice

½ teaspoon (2 ml) fresh
    ground ginger
1 garlic clove, minced
Cherry tomatoes

Cut lamb into 2-inch (5 cm) cubes. Drain pineapple juice into bowl. Reserve chunks. Mix pineapple juice with soy sauce, lemon juice, ginger and garlic. Marinate lamb cubes in mixture for 2 to 3 hours. Put lamb on skewers, alternating with pineapple chunks and tomatoes. Broil over charcoal about 10 minutes turning and basting with marinade. Makes 6 servings.

BUTTERFLY LAMB BARBECUE

1 leg of lamb, about 6 pounds
    (2.7 kg)
2 cups (500 ml) oil
½ cup (125 ml) wine vinegar
2 teaspoons (10 ml) dried rosemary

2 teaspoons (10 ml) salt
1 garlic clove, mashed
Fresh ground pepper to taste

Have meat man bone leg of lamb. (Save bone for soup.) Flatten meat. (It takes a butterfly shape.) Combine remaining ingredients and pour over lamb in a large flat pan. Marinate overnight in refrigerator turning lamb once or twice. Remove from marinade. Broil over charcoal for about 30–45 minutes, turning and brushing with marinade. Makes 6 servings.

117

CALIFORNIA BARBECUE

4 broiler-fryers, 1½ pounds
  each (0.675 kg)
1 teaspoon (5 ml) salt
Fresh ground pepper to taste
1 teaspoon (5 ml) dried oregano
½ cup (125 ml) butter or margarine

3 or 4 sprigs of fresh mint,
  crushed
2 garlic cloves, crushed
¾ cup (180 ml) fresh lemon
  juice
¼ cup (50 ml) chopped parsley

Split chickens. Wash and dry. Rub with salt, pepper and oregano. Melt butter and blend remaining ingredients. Baste chickens and use as a basting sauce while chickens are being broiled over charcoal. Makes 8 servings.

CHICKEN PIECES, BELMONT

½ cup (125 ml) brown sugar,
  firmly packed
½ cup (125 ml) granulated sugar
1 cup (250 ml) all purpose
  barbecue sauce

½ cup (125 ml) soy sauce
¼ cup (50 ml) vinegar
Fresh ground pepper to taste
6 pounds (2.7 kg) frying
  chicken pieces

Combine all ingredients except chicken in saucepan. Heat until sugar is dissolved. Marinate chicken pieces 4 hours or overnite in sauce. Grill chicken over charcoal until tender, about 45 minutes, turning frequently. Brush with sauce last 15 minutes of cooking. Makes 6 to 8 servings.

TOMATO BARBECUE SAUCE

1 large onion, finely chopped
3 tablespoons (45 ml) vinegar
3 tablespoons (45 ml) Worcestershire sauce
1½ teaspoons (7.5 ml) chili powder

1¼ cups (300 ml) water
1¼ cups (300 ml) catsup
1½ teaspoons (7.5 ml) salt

Combine all ingredients in a saucepan. Bring to a boil, cover and simmer about 40 minutes. Store in refrigerator. Use as a basting sauce for pork, beef or lamb. Makes 2 cups (500 ml).

RED WINE MARINADE

1 cup (250 ml) dry red wine
1 cup (250 ml) oil
2 cloves garlic, mashed
1 large onion, finely chopped
1 teaspoon (5 ml) salt

1 teaspoon (5 ml) dried marjoram
1 teaspoon (5 ml) dried thyme
2 teaspoons (10 ml) sugar
2 tablespoons (30 ml) wine
  vinegar

Combine all ingredients and chill several hours before using. Use as a marinade and brush on sauce for beef, lamb or ham steaks. Makes 2½ cups (625 ml). Will keep in refrigerator for several weeks.

WHITE WINE MARINADE

1 cup (250 ml) dry white wine
½ cup (125 ml) lemon juice
1 cup (250 ml) oil
1 tablespoon (15 ml) sugar
1 tablespoon (15 ml) salt

¼ teaspoon (1 ml) dried thyme
¼ teaspoon (1 ml) dried rosemary
¾ cup (180 ml) finely chopped onion
1 clove garlic, mashed
Fresh ground pepper to taste

Combine all ingredients and chill for several hours before using. Use as a marinade and brush on sauce for veal, pork or chicken. Makes 3 cups (750 ml). Will keep in refrigerator for several weeks.

SPREAD ON BARBECUE SAUCE

1 cup (250 ml) softened butter
  or margarine
1 teaspoon (5 ml) dry mustard
1 teaspoon (5 ml) salt
1 teaspoon (5 ml) paprika
1 garlic clove, mashed
1 tablespoon (15 ml) sugar

2 tablespoons (30 ml) lemon juice
2 tablespoons (30 ml) vinegar
2 tablespoons (30 ml) grated onion
2 tablespoons (30 ml) Worcestershire sauce
1 tablespoon catsup
Tabasco sauce to taste

Mix all ingredients together in an electric mixer until well blended. Use as a brush on for ground beef patties, cubed steaks, London broil, lamb shoulder or sirloin chops. Store, covered, in the refrigerator, but remember to get it out ahead of time to reach spreadable consistency. Makes about 1½ cups (375 ml).

SAUCE FOR STEAK OR GROUND BEEF

½ cup (125 ml) fresh mushrooms
6 anchovy fillets
1 garlic clove, mashed
½ cup (125 ml) oil

1½ cups (375 ml) dry red wine
¼ cup (50 ml) brandy
1 can (6 ounce – 168 gm) tomato paste
Fresh ground pepper to taste

Cook mushrooms, anchovy and garlic in the oil until mushrooms are tender, about 5 minutes. Add remaining ingredients. Bring to a boil, cover and simmer 20 minutes. Serve with barbecued steak or beef. Makes 3 cups (750 ml). Can be stored in refrigerator up to a week.

BAR-B-QUE SAUCE

2 tablespoons (30 ml) oil
1 large onion, minced fine
1 garlic clove, crushed
2 tablespoons (30 ml) chili powder
1 teaspoon (5 ml) dry mustard

2 bay leaves
½ teaspoon (2 ml) dried marjoram
2 cans (8 ounce – 224 gm)
    tomato sauce
¼ cup (50 ml) vinegar
½ cup (125 ml) dry red wine

Heat oil in saucepan and cook onion and garlic until tender. Add remaining ingredients and simmer, covered, 20 minutes. Makes 3 cups (720 ml). Use as a brush on sauce for pork, chicken or beef.

PLATTER-PERFECT COLD CUTS

Cold cut platters can be quite spectacular for entertaining. And if you set them up yourself, you can have all the varieties of meats that you want, plus a few other goodies. And feel like an artist in the process.

Choosing the cold cuts

Probably most of us would first choose those we liked best, but also one must think of one's guests. Are there those who might prefer the less spicy — more bland? Baked ham, plain meat loaf and jellied tongue might be their choices. Then you can intersperse those with a few of the brighter varieties. For a large platter I would suggest at least six varieties. In buying cold cuts plan on ¼ – ⅓ pound per person depending on what other food is on the menu.

Choosing the platter

If you don't have a large china or silver platter don't despair. Even one inexpensive 12-inch (30 cm) pizza pan can be the holder for a platter of cold cuts. Carefully cover the pan with aluminum foil, smoothing it to the contours of the pan. So that it will not slip loose on back, either use freezer tape (the best) or cellophane tape to tape it to the pan.

Designing the platter

If you prefer, you can design your platter around a bowl of potato salad in the center, or if the crowd is large and you prefer to have the salad separate in a large bowl, do so. Start arranging the platter by cold cuts from the outside to the center. Either roll, fold crosswide or catty-corner some of the slices to give the platter a 3rd dimension and also make slices easier to pick up with the serving fork. Keep each kind together, and when you buy the cold cuts, try to get one or two varieties that have a little different texture and color. If you do not have a bowl in the center of the platter, use parsley and some small cherry tomatoes. Leave space between the kinds of cold cuts to put deviled eggs, olives and radish roses.

Garnishes for Cold Cut Platter

Parsley — wash well to remove any dirt and rinse. Shake out as much water as possible. Cut off and discard long stems and imperfect pieces. To keep crisp, wrap parsley in a paper towel and put in a plastic bag. Close with a wire closure and store in the vegetable hydrator.

Radishes — wash and cut off root ends. If radishes have leaves, trim off all but one or two small ones. They can be used plain or made into radish roses by peeling red skin back from root end to leaf end to make petals. Chill in ice water. To keep, remove from ice water and store in plastic bag, tightly closed, in vegetable hydrator.

Olives — both stuffed and black.

Cherry tomatoes — wash well and leave on any stem ends that may be found. (Also tomato slices or wedges.)

Pimiento — can be cut into shapes with small cutters and used to garnish potato salad and cole slaw.

Watercress — it is fragile so buy it as close to the party time as possible. Separate stems and store in a plastic bag, tightly closed, in vegetable hydrator. Do not wash unless there is evidence of dirt.

Celery leaves — sometimes when parsley is hard to find, celery leaves, particularly the greenest ones, make a very pretty garnish.

Lemon slices — cut very thin slices or make twists from lemon peel.

Pickles — anything from tiny gherkins to slices or sticks from big dill pickles can be used. To make pickle fans cut small gherkins in thin slices lengthwise from tip almost to stem end. Spread slices apart like a fan.

Onion rings — red or white.

Spiced crab apples.

Carrot curls — peel carrots and strip lengthwise with a potato peeler to make thin slices. Roll around finger and fasten with toothpick. Chill in ice water. Remove toothpick when ready to use.

Green pepper rings — cut green peppers crosswise in thin rings. Remove any white pith.

Cucumber slices — run tines of a fork down sides of unpeeled cucumber to make marks in cucumber. Cut crosswise into slices. Chill in salted ice water.

Care of the Cold Cut Platter

Once the cold cut platter is arranged ready for the guests' arrival, it should not sit around a warm room. It can be set up early in the morning if it is carefully covered with plastic wrap and refrigerated. Overexposure to air dries out cold cuts.

All foods should be kept carefully refrigerated until time to serve. If the weather is hot and guests are likely to be coming over a period of time, it is wise to make 2 or more smaller platters and keep them under refrigeration until needed.

POTATO SALAD

3 medium-sized potatoes
2 eggs
3 tablespoons (45 ml) oil
2 tablespoons (30 ml) vinegar
½ teaspoon (2 ml) salt
Fresh ground pepper to taste

1 small onion, grated
¾ cup (180 ml) finely diced
  celery
½ cup (125 ml) finely diced
  garlic dill pickles
½ cup (125 ml) mayonnaise, about

Scrub potatoes well. Put in a saucepan large enough to also hold eggs. Cover with water, bring to a boil. Cover and simmer. At the end of 15 minutes remove eggs and cool eggs in cold water. Continue cooking potatoes until just tender, about 10 minutes longer.

Peel hot potatoes and dice into bowl. Add oil, vinegar, salt, pepper and grated onion. Mix well. Peel eggs and chill with potatoes. Cover and refrigerate to chill well, at least 3 hours. (Can be overnight). Before ready to serve fold in chopped eggs and remaining ingredients. If necessary add more mayonnaise. Makes about 1 quart (1000 ml).

DEVILED EGGS

6 hard cooked eggs, shelled
5 tablespoons (75 ml) dairy
  sour cream
3 tablespoons (45 ml) prepared
  mustard

1 teaspoon (5 ml) fresh grated
  orange peel
¼ teaspoon (1 ml) dill weed
¼ teaspoon (1 ml) salt
Fresh ground pepper to taste

Cut eggs in half lengthwise. Carefully remove yolks and mash or put through strainer. Blend in remaining ingredients. Fill egg whites with yolk mixture. Chill. If desired garnish with parsley, pimiento or sliced olives. Makes 12 halves.

COLE SLAW

½ cup (125 ml) mayonnaise
2 tablespoons (30 ml) vinegar
1 small onion, grated
½ teaspoon (2 ml) celery seed
1 teaspoon (5 ml) sugar
½ teaspoon (2 ml) salt

Fresh ground pepper to taste
3½ cups (875 ml) crisp
  shredded cabbage
½ cup (125 ml) coarsely shredded carrots
2 tablespoons (30 ml) chopped
  green pepper

Mix mayonnaise with vinegar, onion, celery seed, sugar, salt, pepper. Combine cabbage, carrot and green pepper in a bowl. Add mayonnaise mixture and toss lightly to blend. Chill. Makes about 1 quart.

THE WAYS OF THE WORLD
WITH FOOD

The United States was, is and probably always will be a melting pot for people from other nations, so that many ethnic recipes have become a part of our cuisine. A few like Sauerbraten have survived relatively intact. Others become more submerged in our general cooking, such as the hamburger, and bear only an indistinct impression of their origins.

We are such a large country (Utah is the size of Italy, New Jersey the size of Switzerland) that we have regional cooking as well as ethnic. Regional cooking is based on foods raised along with a congregation of one particular group of persons in a particular area.

The dishes we present here are only a tip of the iceberg in this classification, and since anything ethnic or regional always causes great discussion — we only suggest that these are our versions, culled from many sources.

BEEF STROGANOFF

Beef Stroganoff is of Russian origin. It is another dish for which the ingredients may be gotten ready early in the day, but last minute cooking is a must. Serve with cucumbers vinagrette.

1 pound (0.45 kg) fillet mignon
Salt and fresh ground pepper
   to taste
¼ cup (50 ml) butter
¼ cup (50 ml) flour
1 tablespoon (15 ml) tomato juice
1½ cups (375 ml) beef stock
   or condensed bouillon

1 cup (250 ml) mushrooms thinly
   sliced
½ cup (125 ml) thinly sliced
   onion
½ cup (125 ml) dairy sour cream
Hot cooked noodles

Put fillet mignon in freezer for about one hour to partially freeze and with a sharp knife cut into strips about ¼-inch (0.625 cm) thick. Sprinkle with salt and pepper and let stand for 30 minutes or longer.

Heat 2 tablespoons (30 ml) of butter in a skillet, add flour and brown. Add tomato juice and stock and cook and stir until mixture boils.

Heat remaining butter in another skillet. Quickly brown steak, onions and mushrooms. Add to sauce and simmer 4 to 5 minutes. Stir in sour cream and heat. Do not boil. Taste for seasoning. Serve with hot cooked noodles. Makes 4 servings.

SAUERBRATEN

There are many schools of thought for this recipe. You will find recipes using red wine and those using vinegar. I have chosen a vinegar recipe because it seemed more authentic with the original German recipe. Some even question using gingersnaps, but they are in this version. Boiled potatoes and carrots and dark rye bread compliment sauerbraten.

4 pounds (1.8 kg) beef chuck
  or rump
1 onion, sliced
3 bay leaves
½ teaspoon (2 ml) salt
2 tablespoons (30 ml) sugar
1 teaspoon (5 ml) whole peppercorns

2 cups (500 ml) vinegar
2 cups (500 ml) water
2 tablespoons (30 ml) oil
¼ cup (50 ml) brown sugar
¼ cup (50 ml) raisins
4 to 6 gingersnaps

Put beef into a deep glass or enamel bowl. Add onion, bay leaves, salt, sugar and peppercorns. Heat vinegar and water together and pour over beef. Cover bowl and refrigerate 2 to 4 days (depending on how "sour" you like the meat). Remove meat from marinade. Dry well. Heat oil in Dutch oven and brown meat on all sides. Add onion and 1 cup of the marinade. Bring to a boil, cover and simmer for about 3 hours or until tender. Add more marinade if necessary. When meat is tender, remove from Dutch oven, place on platter and let stand 15 minutes. Meanwhile strain liquid (add more strained marinade to make 2 cups (500 ml) skim off fat. Add brown sugar, raisins and gingersnaps and cook until thickened and smooth. Slice meat and serve with hot gravy. Makes 10 servings.

Meat, poultry, fish, eggs, milk and cheese supply necessary amounts of all essential amino acids.

SUKIYAKI

This Japanese dish is a happy way to cook at the table. An electric skillet is ideal. The beauty of the platter of raw food is part of the pleasure. Serve a light soup first and a fruit dessert.

1½ pounds (0.675 kg)
   sirloin steak cut 1-inch thick
4 stalks celery
2 onions, sliced lengthwise
1 bunch green onions
1 cup (250 ml) mushrooms
½ pound (224 gm) fresh
   spinach

1 can (8½-ounce − 238 gm)
   bamboo shoots, drained
½ cup (125 ml) soy sauce
3 tablespoons (45 ml) white wine
5 tablespoons (75 ml) water
1 tablespoon (15 ml) sugar
1 tablespoon (15 ml) butter or
   margarine
Hot boiled rice

Put steak in freezer for about one hour to partially freeze and with a sharp knife, cut into paper-thin slices. Arrange down the center of a 12-inch round or oblong platter. Cover with saran and refrigerate.

Wash celery and cut diagonally into ½-inch slices. Clean green onions and slice both green and white parts into 2-inch lengths. Wash mushrooms and thinly slice. Wash spinach, cut off stems and steam 1 minute in a colander over boiling water. Arrange vegetables in rows on either side of meat. This can be done early in the day, the platter covered with plastic wrap and refrigerated.

Combine soy sauce, wine, water and sugar in a small pitcher.

When ready to cook, set skillet at 260°F (125°C) and add butter. When butter is melted add ⅓ of the meat and pour ⅔ of the sauce over the meat in the skillet. Add ⅔ of the assorted vegetables to the skillet. Cook and stir gently about 6 minutes. Add another third of the meat and cook 2 − 3 minutes longer. Serve into bowls or small plates. Add remainder of meat and vegetables and sauce as needed for moisture. Cook 7 minutes, stirring, for "extras". Serve with hot cooked rice. Makes 4 servings.

MOUSSAKA

Moussaka, a Greek dish, like so many national dishes, has as many recipes as those who make it. This is a reasonably correct facsimile and very good. A Greek salad with lettuce, cucumbers, black olives will be a good accompaniment.

1 medium size egg plant
1 teaspoon (5 ml) salt
¼ cup (50 ml) flour
4 tablespoons (60 ml) olive oil
4 tablespoons (60 ml) butter or
  margarine
1 cup (250 ml) finely chopped onion
1 pound (0.45 kg) ground lamb
1 pound (0.45 kg) ground beef
1 can (1 pound (448 gm) tomatoes

1 can (6 ounce − 168 gm) tomato
  paste
⅛ teaspoon (0.5 ml) dried oregano
Fresh ground pepper
¼ teaspoon (1 ml) cinnamon
1 cup (250 ml) dry red wine
2 tablespoons (30 ml) butter or
  margarine
3 tablespoons (45 ml) flour
2 cups (500 ml) milk
1 cup (250 ml) grated Parmesan
  cheese

Peel egg plant and slice crosswise into thin slices. Sprinkle with salt and let stand one hour. Dip in ¼ cup (50 ml) flour and brown on both sides in hot olive oil. Drain on paper towels.

Heat 4 tablespoons (60 ml) butter in skillet and cook onion until lightly browned. Add lamb and beef and brown, stirring so it is crumbly. Add tomatoes, tomato paste, oregano, pepper, cinnamon and wine and stir to blend. Cook slowly uncovered until almost all the liquid is absorbed.

Melt 2 tablespoons (30 ml) butter in saucepan. Add 3 tablespoons (45 ml) flour and stir to blend. Stir in milk and cook and stir until mixture boils and is thickened.

Butter a 2½ quart (2.375 L) casserole and arrange half of the egg plant slices in bottom. Add ground beef mixture and cover with remaining egg plant slices. Pour sauce over all. Sprinkle with cheese. Bake at 400°F. (200°C) 1 hour or until top is nicely browned. Let stand 15 − 20 minutes before serving. Makes 6 − 8 servings.

Would you believe that pizzas evolved in Italy from using left over dough? Some evolvement when you think of their popularity. Ours is one version. There are many.

Dough:

2½ to 3 cups (625 – 750 ml)
   all purpose flour
1½ teaspoons (7.5 ml) sugar
2 teaspoons (10 ml) salt

1 package active dry yeast
1 cup (250 ml) very hot tap water
2 tablespoons (30 ml) oil

In a large bowl, thoroughly mix 1 cup (250 ml) flour, sugar, salt and dry yeast. Gradually add very hot tap water and oil to flour mixture and beat 1-minute on low speed of electric mixer, scraping bowl. Stir in enough additional flour to make a soft dough. Turn out on a lightly floured board and knead until smooth and elastic — 8 to 10 minutes. Place in an oiled bowl and turn to oil top. Cover and let rise in a warm place, free from draft, until doubled in bulk, about 45 minutes. Punch dough down, divide into 2 parts and roll each out on a lightly floured board in a circle to fit 2 oiled 12-inch (30 cm) pizza pans. Pull dough to fit pan and to make a standing rim.

Fillings:

2 tablespoons (30 ml) oil
1 cup (250 ml) chopped onion
3 cups (750 ml) canned Italian
   tomatoes
1½ teaspoons (7.5 ml) dried oregano
Fresh ground pepper to taste

1 pound (0.45 kg) pepperoni
   sausage
½ pound (0.225 kg) Mozzarella
   cheese
1 cup (250 ml) fresh grated
   Parmesan cheese

Heat oil and saute onion until tender. Add tomatoes, 1 teaspoon (5 ml) oregano and pepper and cook about 10 minutes. When dough is risen and crusts are formed, cut pepperoni into thin slices crosswise and divide between 2 pizza shells. Cut Mozzarella cheese into small cubes and divide between shells. Spread each with half of tomato sauce and sprinkle with remaining oregano and grated Parmesan cheese. Bake at 425°F (220°C) 20 – 25 minutes or until crusty and browned.

Note: 1 pound (0.45 kg) bulk pork sausage may be used instead of pepperoni. Crumble and brown in skillet. Pour off fat and spread on pizza shells instead of pepperoni.

SWEDISH MEATBALLS

Place meatballs in a hot, deep dish and pour gravy over, to serve. Also have boiled potatoes, pickled gherkins and lingonberries or cranberries.

1 tablespoon (15 ml) butter
3 tablespoons (45 ml) chopped onion
½ cup (125 ml) dried bread crumbs
¾ cup (180 ml) light cream
¼ cup (50 ml) water
½ pound (0.225 kg) ground veal

¼ pound (0.1125 kg) ground beef
¼ pound (0.1125 kg) ground
 fresh pork
1 egg
1 teaspoon (5 ml) salt
¼ teaspoon (1 ml) white pepper

Melt 1 tablespoon (15 ml) butter in skillet and saute onions until golden brown. Soak bread crumbs in cream and water. Add meat, egg, onion, salt and pepper and mix thoroughly until smooth. Shape into balls using 2 tablespoons (30 ml) dipped in cold water. Fry in butter until evenly browned, shaking pan continously to keep balls round. Remove each batch to saucepan and keep hot. Clear skillet in between, before starting next, saving pan juice. When all meatballs are browned, mix flour and cream, add to pan juice and cook and stir until mixture boils and is thickened. If too thick add more milk. Season to taste.

Note: ½ pound (0.225 kg) ground beef   may be substituted for meats specified
        ½ pound (0.225 kg) ground fresh pork

WIENER SCHNITZEL

Duchess potatoes and summer squash, a salad of spiced apple rings to finish the menu.

2 pounds (0.9 kg) thinly sliced
 veal cut from leg
¼ cup (50 ml) flour
1 teaspoon (5 ml) salt
Fresh ground pepper to taste
2 egg yolks
¼ cup (50 ml) milk
½ cup (125 ml) fine dry bread crumbs

¼ cup (50 ml) oil
1 lemon, thinly sliced
6 pitted black olives
6 flat anchovies
Capers
2 eggs, hardcooked and white and
 yolk grated separately

Pound the veal with a mallet between 2 pieces of wax paper so it is very thin. Mix flour with salt and pepper and dip pieces of veal in flour. Mix egg yolks with milk. Dip floured veal in egg yolks and then in bread crumbs. Heat oil in skillet and brown veal quickly on both sides. As browned, place on a hot platter and keep warm. When all veal is browned, arrange in six servings and garnish each as follows: Place a thin slice of lemon on veal, then an olive on the lemon and an anchovy around the olive. Sprinkle with capers and grated whites and yolks of egg. Makes 6 servings.

VEAL PAPRIKAS

Of Hungarian origin, a simple yet delicious way of serving veal. Besides the rice serve pickled beets and steamed cabbage.

6 slices bacon
6 veal cutlets
1 teaspoon (5 ml) salt
Fresh ground pepper to taste

1 cup (250 ml) hot water
1 tablespoon (15 ml) paprika
1 cup (250 ml) dairy sour cream
Hot cooked rice

Cut bacon slices in half and cook until crisp and keep warm. Pan fry the veal cutlets in the bacon grease until nicely browned. Pour off fat. Season cutlets with salt and pepper. Add water and paprika and bring to a boil. Simmer covered, until cutlets are tender, 45 minutes to 1 hour. Remove cutlets to platter. Stir in sour cream. Heat. Do not boil. Serve cutlets with bacon, rice and sour cream gravy. Makes 6 servings.

NEW ENGLAND BOILED DINNER

4 pounds (1.81 kg) corned beef
6 potatoes, peeled
6 carrots, peeled

12 small onions, peeled
1 large head cabbage

Cook corned beef as directed. Remove from broth. Add potatoes, carrots, onions and cabbage. Cook 30 minutes or until vegetables are tender.

Slice corned beef crosswise of the grain and serve 2 slices with a potato, carrot, 2 small onions and a wedge of cabbage for each serving. Always serve mustard, horseradish and vinegar with a New England Boiled Dinner. Makes 6 servings.

CREAMED CHIPPED BEEF AND MUSHROOMS

From Pennsylvania's mushroom country comes this recipe.

½ pound (0.225 kg) dried beef,
   cut up
4 tablespoons (60 ml) butter or
   margarine
3 tablespoons (45 ml) finely chopped
   onion

¼ cup (50 ml) flour
2 cups (500 ml) milk
1 tablespoon (15 ml) chopped parsley
½ teaspoon (2 ml) paprikas
2 tablespoons (30 ml) dry sherry wine
1 can (6-ounce–168 gm) sliced
   mushrooms, drained

Cook beef in butter until until lightly browned. Add onion and cook until tender. Stir in flour and slowly add milk, stirring constantly. Cook and stir until mixture boils and is thickened. Add remaining ingredients and reheat. Serve over hot waffles or toast. Makes 4 to 6 servings.

BEEF TACOS

From the Southwest, a heritage of our closeness to Mexico.

1 pound (0.45 kg) ground beef
1 tablespoon (15 ml) oil
1 medium onion, chopped
1 medium tomato, peeled and chopped
1 teaspoon (5 ml) salt
1 clove garlic, mashed

2 teaspoons (10 ml) chili powder
   (or more, if desired)
8 tortillas or taco shells
Monterey Jack cheese, shredded
Crisp shredded lettuce
Tomato wedges

Saute beef in oil until lightly browned. Add onion and tomato and continue cooking until onion is tender. Stir in salt, garlic and chili powder and cook several minutes more.

Heat tortillas or taco shells as directed on package. First put in the cooked beef. Then add a little cheese, then lettuce and a tomato wedge. Repeat for each tortilla or taco. Makes 8.

"TEXAS" HASH

All that is needed with Texas hash is a bit of greens.

½ pound (0.225 kg) ground fresh
   pork
1 pound (0.45 kg) ground beef
1 cup (250 ml) chopped onion
½ cup (125 ml) chopped green
   pepper
½ cup (125 ml) chopped celery
2 teaspoons (10 ml) chili powder

1 teaspoon (5 ml) salt
Fresh ground pepper to taste
2 cups (500 ml) canned tomatoes
1 can (12 ounce − 336 gm) whole
   kernel corn
½ cup (125 ml) chopped ripe
   olives
½ cup (125 ml) long cooking rice

Brown pork and beef in large skillet. Add remaining ingredients and simmer 30−40 minutes, stirring occasionally. Add water if additional liquid is needed toward end of cooking period. Makes 4 to 6 servings.

CALIFORNIA SHERRY WALNUT HAM

1 canned ham (5 pounds − 2.25 kg)
1 cup (250 ml) brown sugar, firmly
   packed
2 teaspoons (10 ml) dry mustard

4 tablespoons (60 ml) dry sherry
¾ cup (180 ml) chopped walnuts

Heat ham according to directions on label (or about 2 hours at 325°F (160°C). Mix brown sugar with remaining ingredients and spread on ham about 30 minutes before it is done. Spoon drippings from pan over ham while it bakes. Makes 15 to 20 servings.

Minerals essential to growth are found in meat.

SNAPPY RIB BARBECUE

A bowl of potato salad and sliced tomatoes will make this a memorable menu.

3 pounds (1.35 kg) fresh pork
    spareribs
¼ cup (50 ml) catsup
¼ cup (50 ml) soy sauce

¼ cup (50 ml) honey
1 cup (250 ml) chicken broth
2 cloves garlic, crushed
1 teaspoon (5 ml) salt

Have meat man crack spareribs if necessary. Place spareribs in a large flat pan. Leave whole. Mix remaining ingredients and pour over spareribs. Let marinate several hours or overnight in refrigerator. Remove from sauce and barbecue over charcoal coals about 4-inches (10 cm) away from source of heat, turning and brushing with marinade until spareribs are well browned (about 30 minutes). Cut between ribs to serve. Makes 6 servings.

NEW ORLEANS RED BEANS AND RICE

¾ pound (0.3375 kg) dried red kidney
    beans
½ pound (0.225 kg) salt pork or
    ham hock
1 tablespoon (15 ml) bacon fat
1 tablespoon (15 ml) flour
1 large onion, chopped
1 carrot, sliced

1½ quarts (1.425 L) beef bouillon
3 sprigs parsley
1 bay leaf
⅛ teaspoon (0.5 ml) thyme
⅛ teaspoon (0.5 ml) cumin
1 cup (250 ml) sliced celery leaves
3 cups (750 ml) hot cooked rice

Pick over and wash beans. Soak overnight in cold water. If salt pork is used, cut up into ¼-inch squares and brown in skillet. (If ham hock is used, remove from bean mixture when tender, cut off meat and return to beans.) Stir in flour and lightly brown onion. Add carrots, beans, and bouillon to pork. Bring to a boil and simmer covered for about 1 hour. Add parsley, bay leaf, thyme, cumin and celery. Continue cooking until gravy is thick and dark. Check for seasoning. Serve with hot rice. Makes 4 servings.

A meal in one. Serve a tossed salad or a big bowl of finger relishes.

4 tablespoons (50 ml) butter or
  margarine
1 pound (0.45 kg) ham, cubed
3 large onions, chopped
2 garlic cloves, minced
1 pound (0.45 kg) pepperoni or
  Kielbasa thinly sliced
2 large green peppers, seeded and
  chopped
1 can (16 ounce–448 gm) peeled
  tomatoes
1 can (6 ounce – 170 gm) tomato paste
1 cup (250 ml) bouillon

1 teaspoon (5 ml) salt
Fresh ground pepper to taste
½ teaspoon (2 ml) dried thyme
1 stalk celery, chopped
  (including top)
½ cup (125 ml) chopped parsley
1 bay leaf
3 cups (0.75 L) water
1½ cups (375 ml) long cooking
  rice
1 pound (0.45 kg) raw shrimp,
  peeled and deveined

In a heavy skillet or Dutch oven heat butter. Add ham, onions and garlic. Cook and stir to brown onions lightly. Add pepperoni, green peppers, tomatoes, tomato paste, bouillon, salt, pepper, thyme, celery, parsley and bay leaf. Cover and simmer about 1 hour. Remove bay leaf.

Add water and rice and continue cooking about 20 minutes or until rice is tender. Add shrimp and cook 5 minutes longer. Mixture should be relatively dry. Makes 6 servings.

Meat is the richest in phosphorus, the mineral which works with calcium to form strong bones and teeth.

STUFFED HAM

A Mississippi ham to grace a cold board. This recipe, via a famous Inn, would star front stage center of a buffet.

1 ham, 10 – 12 pounds (4.5 – 5.4 kg), not pre-cooked
1 tablespoon (15 ml) vinegar
2 tablespoons (30 ml) brown sugar

Cut off ham hock. Put ham on a rack in a large pan that can be covered. Add water to just come up to the bottom of the ham and put in the vinegar and brown sugar. Cover and steam ham until tender enough so that the bone is loose and can be removed. Remove bone and all fat from ham. Stuff ham with dressing and cover outside of ham with remainder. Tie tightly in cheese cloth and bake at 300°F. (145°C) for ½ hour. Chill 24 hours. Remove cheesecloth and slice very thin to serve.

Dressing

1 cup (250 ml) ham fat
1 pound (4.5 kg) toasted soda crackers, ground
12 slices bread, toasted, ground
2 medium onions, ground
2 tablespoons (30 ml) sugar

½ teaspoon (2 ml) dry mustard
½ cup (150 ml) pickle relish
4 eggs, beaten
¼ teaspoon (1 ml) Tabasco sauce
White wine (dry)

Thoroughly combine all ingredients, using enough white wine to make a paste like consistency, but not too soft.

HEARTLAND HAM LOAF

1 egg
½ cup (125 ml) milk
2 tablespoons (30 ml) grated onion
½ teaspoon (2 ml) Worcestershire sauce
½ cup (125 ml) fine cracker crumbs
1 teaspoon (5 ml) salt

Fresh ground pepper to taste
1 pound (0.45 kg) ground beef
½ pound (0.225 kg) ground lean pork
½ pound (0.225 kg) ground cooked ham
Horseradish

Mix egg with milk, onion, Worcestershire sauce, cracker crumbs, salt and pepper. Add meats and mix thoroughly. Pack into a 9 x 5 x 3 inch (22.5 x 12.5 x 7.5 cm) greased loaf pan. Bake at 350°F (175°C) for 1½ hours. Serve with horseradish. Makes 8 servings.

BAKED PORK CHOPS MIDWEST

6 pork chops, 1 inch (2.5 cm) thick
1 teaspoon (5 ml) salt
Fresh ground pepper to taste
1 teaspoon (5 ml) poultry seasoning

2 tablespoons (30 ml) bacon fat
1 cup (250 ml) quick-cooking rice
1 can (10½ ounce – 294 gm) condensed
   cream of chicken soup
1 cup (250 ml) milk

Season pork chops with salt, pepper and poultry seasoning. Brown on both sides in hot bacon fat in a skillet. As browned, transfer to a buttered large flat casserole. Sprinkle rice over chops. Mix soup with milk and pour over rice and pork chops being sure all rice is moistened. Cover tightly. If casserole does not have a lid, cover with aluminum foil. Bake at 350°F. (175°C) for 1¼ hours or until pork chops are tender. Makes 6 servings.

WILLIAMSBURG BRUNSWICK STEW

Serve this old-time stew (many recipes call for squirrel) in deep dishes with lots of bread to sop up the juice.

1 fowl — 6 pounds (2.7 kg)
3 quarts (3 L) water
2 large onions, sliced
2 cups (500 ml) sliced okra
4 cups (1000 ml) canned tomatoes
2 cups (500 ml) fresh or frozen
   lima beans

4 medium potatoes, sliced
4 cups (1000 ml) whole kernel corn
2 teaspoons (10 ml) salt
Fresh ground pepper to taste
1 tablespoon (15 ml) sugar

Cut chicken in 8 pieces and cook in water until tender, about 2 hours. Remove chicken. Add onion, okra, tomatoes, lima beans and potatoes to broth. Simmer about 45 minutes, stirring occasionally. Add additional water if necessary. Remove chicken from bone and dice. Add with corn and seasonings to stew and cook 5 minutes longer. Makes 8 to 10 servings.

Don't preheat the oven for meats, stews or casseroles.

136

KENTUCKY BURGOO

This famous Southern dish is a must on Kentucky Derby Day — plus all the other days important to Kentucky celebrations. It's celebration size in quantity.

2 pounds (0.9 kg) pork shank
4 pounds (1.8 kg) veal shank
2 pounds (1.8 kg) breast of lamb
1 fowl, (4 to 5 pounds (1.8 to 2.25 kg)
7 quarts (6.65 L) water
1 pound (0.45 kg) potatoes, peeled and diced
1 pound (0.45 kg) onions, chopped
5 or 6 carrots, peeled and diced
2 green peppers, seeded and diced
2 cups (500 ml) diced okra
2 stalks celery, diced

2 cups (500 ml) chopped cabbage
2 cups (500 ml) whole kernel corn
2 cups (500 ml) fresh or canned green lima beans
2 pods red pepper, cut up
1 quart (0.95 L) pureed tomatoes
1½ tablespoons (22.5 ml) salt
½ teaspoon (2 ml) Tabasco sauce
2 tablespoons (30 ml) thick steak sauce
1 tablespoon (15 ml) Worcestershire sauce
¾ cup (180 ml) chopped parsley

Put all the meat (including the fowl) in cold water in a 4 to 5 gallon (15.2 to 19 L) pot and bring to boil. Cover and simmer until meat is tender enough to fall off the bone, 2 to 3 hours.

Remove meat from broth. Cool and chop the meat coarsely. Return to broth and add all the vegetables. Cover and simmer until thick, 2 hours or more. It should be thick but still soupy. Add seasonings and toward the end of cooking time check for any additional seasonings to suit personal taste. Stir often and keep heat low as Burgoo gets toward "thick" stage. Add parsley. Serve in bowls or deep plates. Makes about 25 servings.

The body building proteins of meat are completely and easily utilized by the body.

ARROZ CON PUERCO
(RICE WITH PORK)

Southern Floridians have adopted many Spanish (Cuban) dishes and this is one.

2 tablespoons (30 ml) oil
1 clove garlic, finely minced
1 pound (0.45 kg) lean, boneless pork
 shoulder, cubed
1½ pounds (0.675 kg) meaty salt
 pork, diced
1 medium onion, sliced

1 green pepper, seeded and sliced
¾ cup (180 ml) uncooked rice
1 can (1 pound, 13 ounce (812 gm)
 tomatoes
¾ cup (180 ml) cooked peas
¼ cup (50 ml) diced pimiento

Heat oil in skillet and slowly brown garlic and pork over low heat. In another skillet, cook diced salt pork until lightly browned and most of the fat is cooked out. Add onion and green pepper and cook until lightly browned. With a slotted spoon remove the pork, onions and green pepper. Pour off all but about ¼ cup (50 ml) fat and brown rice until golden. Return salt pork, onions, green pepper, pork and tomatoes to skillet. Stir to mix well. Bring to a boil, cover and simmer until all the liquid is absorbed and rice is tender, about 20–30 minutes. Stir in peas and pimiento and let heat a few minutes longer. Taste for seasoning. Makes 4 servings.

VERMONT MEAT PIE

These French-Canadian pies have crept over the border into Vermont and are now a part of that state's heritage.

1 pound (0.45 kg) boneless fresh pork
 shoulder
1 pound (0.45 kg) boneless beef chuck
2 large onions
⅛ teaspoon (0.5 ml) dried thyme
1 teaspoon (5 ml) salt

6 peppercorns
¾ teaspoon cinnamon
¾ teaspoon dried sage
1 cup (250 ml) mashed potatoes
Pastry for 1 9-inch (22.5 cm) double
 crust pie

Put pork, beef, one onion, thyme, salt and peppercorns in a saucepan and cover with water. Bring to a boil. Cover and simmer about 1 hour or until tender enough to fall off bone. Cool and remove fat. Grind meat and remaining onion. Mix with cinnamon, sage and mashed potatoes. If too stiff, add a little broth. Roll out half of pastry and fit into a 9-inch pie plate. Add filling and cover with top crust. Seal edges. Bake at 375°F (190°C) for one hour or until browned. Serve hot or cold, as a main dish or in small wedges for an hors d'ouevres. Makes 1 9-inch pie.

WEST COAST BROILED CHICKEN LIVERS

1 cup (250 ml) dry white wine
½ cup (125 ml) brandy
⅛ teaspoon (0.5 ml) Tabasco sauce
2 tablespoons (30 ml) Worcestershire sauce
8 whole cloves
1 teaspoon (5 ml) caraway seeds
½ teaspoon (2 ml) fresh ground ginger
2 bay leaves

8 whole peppercorns
½ teaspoon (2 ml) salt
Fresh ground pepper to taste
4 tablespoons (60 ml) oil
1½ pounds (0.675 kg) chicken livers
¼ cup (50 ml) butter or
margarine, melted
1 tablespoon cornstarch
3 cups (750 ml) hot cooked rice

Combine wine and brandy with seasonings and oil and bring to a boil. Cook 3 minutes. Pour over chicken livers in a bowl. Cover and refrigerate over night. Stir once or twice.

Remove livers and drain. Strain sauce and measure 1 cup. Put livers on broiler pan, pour melted butter over them and broil 2 to 3 minutes, until lightly browned. Mix cornstarch with cold marinade and heat to boiling, stirring until thickened and clear. Serve with chicken livers and rice. Makes 4 servings.

Use the oven to cook all the individual courses of a meal at once, for example: soup, casserole, main dish and dessert.

METRIC CONVERSION CHART

Length

Multiply inches	x 2.5	to get centimeters	cm
Multiply feet	x 30.0	to get centimeters	cm
Multiply yards	x 0.9	to get meters	m
Multiply miles	x 1.6	to get kilometers	km

Weight

Multiply ounces	x 28	to get grams	gm
Multiply pounds	x 0.45	to get kilograms	kg

Volume

Multiply teaspoons	x 5	to get milliliters	ml
Multiply tablespoons	x 15	to get milliliters	ml
Multiply ounces	x 30	to get milliliters	ml
Multiply cups	x 0.24	to get liters	1
Multiply pints	x 0.47	to get liters	1
Multiply quarts	x 0.95	to get liters	1
Multiply gallons	x 3.8	to get liters	1

Temperature

To change from Fahrenheit to Celsius:
Subtract 32 from Fahrenheit, divide by 9 and multiply by 5. This will give you the Celsius. In Celsius, freezing is 0° – in Fahrenheit it is 32°.

INDEX